The Mallory Library

Make the Most of Your Income

by
John L. Springer

**PRENTICE-HALL, INC.
ENGLEWOOD CLIFFS, N.J.**

McIntire Public Library
Charlottesville, Virginia

332
Springer
1961

cop. 1

Library of Congress Catalog Card Number: 61-10012

© Copyright 1961 by Prentice-Hall Inc., Englewood Cliffs, N.J.

All rights reserved, including the right to reproduce this book, or any portions thereof, in any form, except for the inclusion of brief quotations in a review.

Printed in the United States of America
54587-T

To
ELLEN

Acknowledgments

This volume represents viewpoints and recommendations from many sources, and I am indebted to hundreds of men and women who, in various ways, generously helped in its preparation.

I particularly wish to thank the many persons who, as individuals and representatives of organizations mentioned in the text, gave the benefit of their experience and advice so that this book might truly give its readers the best available guidance. I express my appreciation to Miss Janet Murray, chief of the survey statistics staff, and Miss Eloise Cofer, food economist, of the U.S. Department of Agriculture; Mrs. Alice K. Leopold, assistant to the Secretary of Labor; Victor Christgau, director of the Bureau of Old Age and Survivors Insurance of the Social Security Administration, and Mrs. Charlotte Crenson, information specialist of the Bureau of Old Age and Survivors Insurance; Robert M. Parrish, executive director, and S. F. Stowe, director of the information division, of the Federal Trade Commission.

To Rudolph R. Fichtel and Raymond Chesseldean of the American Bankers Association; Victor H. Nyborg, president, and Thomas C. Roberts, director of public relations, of the Association of Better Business Bureaus, Inc.; Lee F. Block, manager of the public relations division of the Blue Cross Association; Hilton Davis, manager of the Domestic Distribution Department of the Chamber of Commerce of the United States; Rudolph M. Severa, executive manager of the Credit Bureau of Greater New York; Warren P. Lutey, director of the public

Acknowledgment

relations department, Credit Union National Assn.; Robert C. Frese, assistant vice president of the Dime Savings Bank of Brooklyn; Jerry Voorhis, executive director of the Cooperative League of the U.S.A.; Alfred V. Taylor, director of the public relations service of the Family Service Association of America; Larry Eisinger, editor-in-chief of Fawcett Books; Kenneth E. Small, manager of the savings bond department of the Federal Reserve Bank of New York.

To Daniel J. Sullivan, administrative assistant of the Group Health Association, Inc., of Washington, D.C.; James R. Williams, vice president of the Health Insurance Institute; Dr. Ernst A. Dauer, director of consumer credit studies, and Miss Leone Ann Heuer, director of the Money Management Institute, of the Household Finance Corporation; Alfred Cranwill, C.L.U., and Miss Betty S. Martin, director of the women's division, of the Institute of Life Insurance; Mrs. Marion Stevens Eberly, R. Wilfred Kelsey and Arthur C. Daniels, also of the institute; J. Carroll Bateman, general manager, Charles C. Clarke, assistant manager, and Burton L. Youngman, director of research, of the Insurance Information Institute; Frank O. Allison, advertising supervisor of the Massachusetts Indemnity and Life Insurance Company; George Mooney, executive director, and Joseph S. Rosapepe, director of public information, of the National Association of Investment Companies.

To Charles H. Bernhard, assistant director of public relations of the National Association of Real Estate Boards; J. Gordon Dakins, executive vice president of the National Retail Merchants Association; Miss Helen White, executive secretary of the National Thrift Committee; Ruddick C. Lawrence, vice president, and Robert G. Deindorfer, of the department of public information, of the New York Stock Exchange; Miss Mabel Spray, extension specialist in family economics at the Ohio State University.

To Clyde S. Casady, executive vice president of the Savings Bank Association of Massachusetts; Richard A. Peters, assistant

Acknowledgment

secretary of the Savings Bank Life Insurance Council; Norman Strunk, executive vice president, and William B. O'Connell, public relations counsel, of the United States Savings and Loan League; R. A. Seelig, director of information of the United Fresh Fruit and Vegetable Association; John H. Seiter, vice president of the Washington Heights Federal Savings and Loan Association of New York; and Herman H. York, head of his own firm of architects at Jamaica, N.Y.

For permission to quote selections from their works, I thank Professor Arch W. Troelstrup of Stephens College, author of *Consumer Problems and Personal Finance* (copyrighted by McGraw-Hill Book Company, Inc., New York); Professor Frances Lomas Feldman, of the University of Southern California, author of *The Family in a Money World* (copyrighted by the Family Service Association of America); Dr. Paul Popenoe, general director of the American Institute of Family Relations, Los Angeles, author of *Marriage is What You Make It* (copyrighted by the Macmillan Company) and the estate of Dr. John A. Schindler, M.D., author of *How to Live 365 Days a Year* (copyrighted by Prentice-Hall).

Most of all do I acknowledge my gratitude to my wife, Ellen Albright Springer, for her forbearance and encouragement during the year of writing.

JOHN L. SPRINGER.

Scarsdale, N.Y.

Contents

INTRODUCTION   xi

You *Can* Live Better on Your Income. Six Ways to Help You Manage Your Money.

CHAPTER 1. **TO LIVE BETTER YOU NEED A SPENDING PLAN**   1

Seven Steps to a Good Spending Plan. How to Make Your Spending Plan Work.

2. **HOW TO GET THE MOST FOR YOUR MONEY WHEN YOU SHOP**   13

Don't Buy on Impulse. Double-Check Major Purchases. Comparison Shop on Major Items. Buy for Cash and Forego Unnecessary Services. Wait for Special Sales. Learn to Interpret Advertisements. Be a Label Reader. Master These Tricks of Supermarket Shopping. Learn to Detect Gyps.

3. **THE TWO EDGES OF CREDIT**   34

When It's O.K. to Use Credit. Are You a Good Credit Risk? How You Can Buy on Credit. How You Can Borrow Money. How to Figure What Credit Will Cost You. How You Can Keep Out of Trouble With Your Creditors. What About Credit Cards?

4. **HOW TO PUT YOUR EXTRA CASH TO WORK**   55

What Planned Savings Will Do for You. How Much Should You Be Saving? What to Look for Before Opening a Savings Account. Where Should You Place Your Savings? "Investing in America" With Savings Bonds. Five Ways to Be a Successful Saver. How You Can Save Money in a Hurry.

5. **HOW TO PROTECT YOUR FAMILY WITH LIFE INSURANCE**   74

Where You Can Buy Insurance. Six Points to Remember. Who Can Get Social Security Payments.

Contents

6. **COULD YOUR LIFE BE RUINED IN TWENTY SECONDS?**   95

   Automobile Insurance. Home and Personal Property Insurance. Personal Liability Insurance. Title Insurance. Hospital and Health Insurance. Beware of These Trick Clauses in Your Health Policy. Five Points to Remember Before You Buy Hospital or Health Insurance. Your Answer to Sky-Rocketing Medical Bills.

7. **HOW TO USE A CHECKING ACCOUNT**   113

   How to Use Your Checkbook. How Checks Are Processed. What You Should Know About Endorsements. Balancing Your Checkbook. Ten Don'ts to Remember.

8. **A SHORT COURSE IN STOCKS AND BONDS**   121

   What Investing Really Means. What Investment Is Best for You. How to Decide Where to Invest. How the Stock Market Works. Buying and Selling "Over the Counter." Mutual Funds and What They Do. What You Should Know About Automatic Investing Plans. Ten Ways to Avoid Getting Gypped on Stocks and Bonds.

9. **THERE IS AN ART TO BUYING A HOUSE**   141

   What Can You Afford to Pay? Can You Pass th FHA Requirements? What You Should Know About Mortgages. Don't Forget Your Closing Costs. Four Musts to Help You Choose the Right House.

10. **WHAT KIND OF HOUSE IS BEST FOR YOU?**   163

    If You Buy a New House—. Two Rules to Help You Buy a Lot Wisely. Start With a Trailer Home?

11. **DOES YOUR FAMILY REALLY NEED A SECOND INCOME?**   181

    Does It Pay to Take a Second Job? Where Are the Part-Time Jobs for Women? How Can You Go About Getting a Part-Time Job? Before You Start Your Own Business. What You Must Know to Run a Business.

12. **YOU ARE PREPARING FOR RETIREMENT**   198

    Social Security Can't Do It All. You Can "Buy a Steady Income" for Your Declining Years. Three Questions to Answer Before You Buy an Annuity.

INDEX   209

INTRODUCTION

You *Can* Live Better on Your Income

This book will show you how to use one of the most important tools of your life. Money is this tool—one you must use, or at least think about, every day you live. Use it wisely and you can obtain all the necessities for your family—plus comforts and luxuries which make daily living more joyful. Use it poorly and you will be harassed without end—bogged down by expenses you cannot meet, constantly in debt, unable to achieve the sense of security that comes from preparing well for your own future.

This book will help you live better on your present income. It will show you how to earn, save and spend money more successfully. It will help you to a happier marriage and to a more comfortable life. It will aid you in achieving goals—a home for your family, a college education for your children, comfortable retirement for yourself—which all of us dream about but too few achieve.

To help you use your money more effectively, I consulted hundreds of experts throughout the country. They included domestic scientists, investment advisers, officials of banks and savings and loan associations, professors, insurance men. From these contacts, I have found that there are six clear rules for successful money management—six principles you can use to solve the money problems in your life. Here they are:

• *Put money in its proper place.* Despite what many people believe, a wealthy family is not necessarily happier than one which struggles along on a minimum wage. In fact, a family with an annual income of $50,000 might be considerably less happy than one with a tenth of its income.

Dr. Paul Popenoe, general director of the American Institute of Family Relations in Los Angeles, says he has never known of a couple who sought a divorce merely because the husband lost his job or took a heavy cut in salary. In his book, *Marriage Is What You Make It,* he says that "it is not the amount of income, but the agreement on how that amount should be handled, that is significant to marital happiness.

"Where disagreement does exist," he says, "it is likely to become more and more prominent. In short, quarrels over finances rarely make a good marriage bad, but they often make a bad marriage worse."

What is a proper attitude to have about money? Authorities generally agree: You should consider it as a means to an end, not an end in itself.

It cannot buy the most important things—the satisfactions of parenthood, for example, or mutual love, respect, sympathy, understanding. Regardless of their income, a husband and wife must recognize this fact to achieve happiness.

But it will buy many of life's good things—a home, a car, proper medical care, an education for your children. And you are entitled to try to get them.

You will make a tragic mistake if you sacrifice spiritual and emotional values to achieve material success. That kind of success does not bring happiness unless it is accompanied by high ideals.

Accept the fact that money should be your servant, not your master, and you can adopt a more relaxed attitude and keep things in perspective. You will not let thoughts of material gain rule your life, but you will be alert to what intelligent use of your income can do for you.

• *Set up a long-range program.* "Couples who use money effectively know what they want to do with their money over the years and they have taken the most important step to make their program work—they have learned to spend less than they earn," says Norman Strunk, executive vice president of the United States Savings and Loan League.

"Everyone who ever hopes to achieve any degree of financial security must take this step. For only when you master the art of saving will you start to make progress with your long-term program.

"You need savings to achieve a home, a good education for your children, retirement comforts for yourself.

"Finally, you need savings to build your estate—to leave some money to your children after you die, so that they may have a start toward financial security in their own lives.

"In order to build a sound financial foundation for your future, you should clearly understand what you want to do. Do you want to buy a home? Start a business of your own? Pay for your child's college education later? Retire to a sunny climate or travel in your old age? If you know the answers, you will have goals to work for. They will serve as a beacon to help you determine how all your other money is spent."

• *Establish goals you can reach.* Anne Hamilton was a bride of 22, married to an office worker who earned $90 a week. She could not see why they could not afford a summer cottage by the lake. So she rented one at $400 a month. This was entirely out of keeping with the Hamiltons' station and her action kept them in financial hot water for a year while they struggled to pay for it. It was a typical example of how some people fail to be realistic about money.

In his book, *How to Live 365 Days a Year*, Dr. John A. Schindler cites this as a principle to make your life richer: "Don't want what you can't have."

He says:

"A trick for dispelling dissatisfaction is to quit wanting, wanting this, wanting that. I knew a man of moderate means with a large family, who made himself miserable wanting things he couldn't afford. First, he longed for an expensive camera. He worked himself into such an irritation of desire that he finally bought it, although he could ill afford it, and his family could afford it even less. When he had that, he began to fairly itch for a power saw and could think of little else until he had that; next, he had to have a drill press. And so it went on. He was always dissatisfied with what he had and thought he needed more. His family, meanwhile, was deprived of much it really needed.

"It would have been just as easy for this man to have found pleasure in things that it was easier for him to have. His education had been faulty; there had been no one to show him how to find enjoyment without expense."

Couples who calmly decide what they can afford—and what is beyond their means—are better able to achieve success with their money. If you set goals within your reach, you can work effectively to achieve them. If the goals are far beyond you, you will soon be disappointed and discouraged by failure.

Success breeds success in money management as in everything else. Say you succeed in saving for a new car. You will be encouraged to set other goals in the future. You will be able to bear the necessary sacrifices; you will know from experience that achieving your objective will make them worthwhile.

• *Hold regular family money conferences.* In some homes, husband and wife do not discuss the subject of money until a crisis arises—creditors start hounding them for past debts or they have no cash for daily expenses and must try to borrow some at high interest rates. Then the discussion is highly charged with emotion. As often as not, it winds up with mutual charges and recriminations. Where financial problems are well-handled, however, husband and wife often review together what they are doing with their money and consider how to improve their methods of handling it.

If yours is an average family, there will be countless demands upon you to spend. You can buy more clothing, send your children to private schools, trade in your old automobile for a newer model, move to a more expensive neighborhood, take a cross-country trip instead of spending your vacation at a nearby place. But you must realistically accept the fact that if you choose one thing, you will probably have to forego another: Few families can buy a new station wagon and take a trip from New York to California at the same time.

That is why family conferences help husband and wife (and older children) to decide together how the family's money will be spent—and where savings will be made if they are necessary to make another purchase possible.

Your family will lack a sense of purpose unless you agree on how to spend your money. Moreover, lack of planning can damage its financial future. Here is one example:

A husband decided his family should have a cabin cruiser to explore the Great Lakes in summer. His wife decided they needed new living room furniture. Neither consulted the other. He bought the boat and she bought the furniture—both on the installment plan. They were deeply in debt for years.

Mrs. Marion Stevens Eberly, former director of the Women's Division of the Institute of Life Insurance, has commented:

"It is particularly important for people to learn to plan together when they are first married. No bride and husband ever have exactly the same ideas about money. But they can learn to understand each other's views and to compromise. If they are wise, they will start doing it as soon as they can.

"Remember, however, that a man and woman don't spend money the same way. He may shudder when she 'has nothing to wear' while her closet bulges with clothes. She will recoil when he spends as no woman would.

"A young husband and wife would be foolish if they expected their item-for-item expenses to balance. But they can trust each other to live up to the same spending standards. If the family must be extra prudent, he should be allowed to economize in his way and she in hers.

"Young couples must face many questions which have no answers except the ones they can work out together. If Mary has a savings account of her own, should it be pooled or is it her money? If she works, should she and her husband put their incomes together or keep them separate and each be responsible for separate items of family expenditure? If they must choose between the car John wants or the furniture Mary thinks more important, who wins? Only the husband and wife together can answer these questions in a family conference."

• *Keep a close check on how you spend your money.* Columbia University researchers examined 1500 families, separating good money managers from poor ones. They found that good managers had this in common: They knew exactly where their money went. Inefficient managers had only vague notions of the amounts they laid out each week for food, clothing, laundry and other items.

By keeping records of what you spend, you may be able to control a main cause of budget troubles: Impulse spending. One man insisted that his monthly personal expenses amounted to only $40. When he checked, he discovered that he spent more than half that at bars alone. A woman wondered why her food bills were so high. She never fully realized the answer until she analyzed item by item: Almost a fourth of what she spent went for snacks—soft drinks, candies, other things to nibble on—which were not necessary to nourish her family. She had developed a habit of putting them into her shopping-cart on impulse.

If you have not checked up recently, odds are that you spend much more than you imagine on your automobile, entertainment, clothes or in some other area which strikes your fancy. For example, how much does your car cost you? Economists put the average cost—including gas, oil, tires, maintenance, insurance, depreciation—at around $1,000 per year. Most persons guess the cost at about half of that.

While your records should give you a general idea of where

your money goes, you need not live on a rigid budget. You do not have to specify that certain amounts should be spent each week for milk, bread, and so on. But the lower your income, the more important it is that you tightly control your expenses—even down to what you spend for carfare.

• *Learn to discipline yourself.* The roads to hell and the bankruptcy courts are paved with good intentions. You must not only know how to handle your financial problems effectively, you must also have the *will* to do it. "The essence of successful money management," says Professor Frances Lomas Feldman of the University of Southern California, "is the person's capacity to discipline himself into *following* a plan."

Many couples fail financially because they do not discipline themselves. They cannot or will not recognize that everything worthwhile requires sacrifices. When young couples fall into installment debt and remain there for a lifetime, the reason almost always is the same: They lack the ability to make sacrifices. Because they need someone to force them to make monthly payments regularly, they may pay 15 or 20 percent more for everything they buy on the installment plan.

In her book, *The Family in a Money World,* published by the Family Service Association of America, Professor Feldman says that "any plan to maintain solvency of the family involves the co-operation of all members. Keeping solvent is not an easy task. *Often current satisfactions must be given up for future gains.*"

You will constantly encounter temptations to buy items you do not really need. Therefore, you must learn to keep your eye on your major objectives and to say "no" to other things. Remember: To get the important things tomorrow, you must resist the urge to splurge on less important things today.

Six Ways to Help You Manage Your Money

If you want to manage your family's money in a way that contributes to your security and peace of mind, remember these six principles:

1. Put money in its proper place. It is a tool to help you gain your objectives—not a goal in itself.

2. Set up a long-range program. Keep in mind the big things you want to do with your money in the future.

3. Establish goals you can reach. Don't waste time striving for things far beyond your grasp.

4. Hold regular family money conferences. Agree with your mate how you will spend and save your income.

5. Keep a close check on your expenditures. You may be surprised at how much is leaking out in impulse spending and in other ways.

6. Discipline yourself. Learn to say "no" to temptations that would detour you from your main goals.

chapter one

TO LIVE BETTER, YOU NEED A SPENDING PLAN

No matter what you earn, you must learn to keep expenses below your income

Whether you earn a million dollars a year or work for minimum wages, you share a common problem: You must learn to live within your income. Even a millionaire may be unable to afford a seagoing yacht and a summer home in the North and a winter home in the South and a year 'round penthouse apartment on Park Avenue. He cannot have everything he wants. Unless he carefully decides how to spend his money, he will soon be bankrupt.

So it is with the rest of us. We could all easily spend twice as much as we earn. From all sides we are urged to do so: Buy a new car or new home, take a cruise, replace last year's clothes with this year's styles, put a swimming-pool in the back yard, send our child to summer camp. If we do not choose from among the things we are urged to buy, we too will be hopelessly in debt.

That is why you need a spending plan if you are to handle your finances wisely. You should clearly understand how much you can afford for various items you need or want. This spending plan need not be a formal thing in black and white. Millions of families manage successfully without a "budget." The important point—on which virtually all authorities agree—

is to understand precisely where you want your money to go.

"Only you can decide how you should spend your income," says Mabel Spray, extension specialist in family economics at Ohio State University. "The spending plan for each family depends on income, the size and age of its members, where they live, what they do, and what kind of responsibilities they have.

"Before a family can improve its spending plan, it must have pretty well in mind the goals or aims it wants to reach sometime in the future. Some goals need to be stated as long-time goals; others may be immediate. They may be better food, a more attractive and convenient house, more family celebrations and parties with friends and neighbors, education for children, travel, contributions to church or a variety of other goals."

Regardless of our long-range objectives, however, all of us have the same basic expenses to which we must allot a certain percentage of our incomes.

SHELTER: Leone Ann Heuer, director of the Money Management Institute of Household Finance Corporation, says that how much you spend will depend to a large extent on:

How important you consider the physical aspects of your home. Some people obtain most of their satisfaction in living around it. Others prefer to spend less on housing and more for special interests like education, travel, music, hobbies or sports.

Number and ages of your children and whether you want a house with a yard that is conveniently accessible to good schools.

What your income will allow. Whether you rent or make payments on a house you have bought or built, you will have to make regular payments—usually monthly—on a specific date.

Miss Heuer says that other costs as well as rent or mortgage payments must be included in your shelter allowance. To determine what shelter now costs you, jot down what you spend

To Live Better, You Need a Spending Plan

annually for any of the following items which would apply to your situation:

	Annual Cost
Rent	_____
Mortgage payment (including interest)	_____
Property taxes (if not part of your mortgage payment)	_____
Property insurance (if not part of your mortgage payment)	_____
Fuel for heating	_____
Utilities (gas, electricity, telephone, water)	_____
Services (garbage collections, paid help to maintain house and yard, etc.)	_____
Costs of repairs, redecorating, or remodeling— (Average is 1 to 3 percent of the total cost of your house.)	_____
Other shelter costs not included above	_____
TOTAL—	_____

To determine your shelter costs per month, divide the above total by 12.

FOOD: Regardless of your income, you should provide good, nourishing food for every member of the family. To do this, there is a point of spending for food below which you should not go. Families in low-income groups generally spend a higher percentage of their wages on food than do those in upper brackets. For example, one published budget shows that a family of four (husband, wife, two children) with take-home pay of $500 per month might allow about $90 per month for food. A family of the same size with monthly take-home income of $700 might allow $110. One with an income of $1,000 might allow $150.

Here is a low-cost weekly food plan prepared by the staff of the Institute of Home Economics, U. S. Department of Agriculture. It is designed to provide good nutrition for $20 to $22 a week (based on 1960 prices) for a couple and two children under 6. You can use it as a base, and spend more on tastier foods, juicier cuts of meat and more appealing desserts if you can afford it.

Milk, cheese, ice cream (milk equivalent)	18 quarts
Meat, poultry, fish	9 pounds
Eggs	1¾ dozen
Dry beans and peas, nuts	¾ to 1 pound
Grain products	9 to 10 pounds
Citrus fruit, tomatoes	7½ pounds
Dark green and deep yellow vegetables	2 pounds
Potatoes	7 to 7½ pounds
Other vegetables and fruits	16 pounds
Fats, oils	1½ pounds
Sugars, sweets	2 pounds

The lower your allowance, the more important is it that you buy the least expensive foods in each group that are high in food value and that you shop carefully to get more for your money. The next chapter contains many tested suggestions to help you.

LIFE INSURANCE: Most young couples probably cannot afford as much as they should have. Richard A. Peters of the Savings Bank Life Insurance Council of Massachusetts says that in such cases the bulk of the money available for insurance premiums should be used to buy life insurance on the breadwinner's life. For most young husbands, the choice must be from among the low-cost types of policy, e.g., term insurance, straight life, or a "family income" policy which combines straight life with decreasing term insurance.

He says: "It is important to keep flexibility in mind when working out your program, because your needs for life insurance will change during your lifetime. There are three general stages:

"Early years of marriage (years 1 through 20 or 25). Your children are growing up, the mortgage is outstanding and your income has not reached its peak. This is usually when you need life insurance the most.

"Middle years (year 25 through retirement). Your children become self-supporting, your mortgage is usually paid off, your income reaches its peak. Your need for insurance is no longer so great. The emphasis shifts to funds to supplement your retirement income.

"Retirement (age 65 on). Now you may merely need enough life insurance to meet final expenses. In some cases there may be such considerations as taxes and income for the surviving spouse. Any insurance after retirement should be on a paid-up basis, because all your retirement income will probably be needed to meet everyday living expenses."

In view of the fact that your needs change, how much you might spend on insurance depends upon individual circumstances. But there are dangers in buying more insurance than you can reasonably afford. For instance, if you have difficulty making the payments, you may be tempted to drop the entire program. Then your family will lack any security.

Some young couples, in a burst of zeal, over-buy insurance. But soon they let their policies lapse. After this experience, they become insurance-shy. They fear buying additional policies, realizing that what has happened once can be repeated. So they go through life without any protection.

MEDICAL CARE AND INSURANCE: According to James R. Williams, vice president of the Health Insurance Institute, about five percent of the average family's take-home pay goes to pay medical care bills, including health insurance premiums.

Part of this amount should cover ordinary doctor, dentist and pharmacy bills and other expenses. Part should provide for a health insurance program which would help meet doctor-hospital bills and at the same time protect your family from big bills resulting from a really serious illness or accident.

Mr. Williams says that you should budget more than five percent, however, if you expect maternity expenses. The maternity benefits in hospital insurance policies vary greatly. Some provide a lump sum payment toward meeting maternity costs. Others pay the full costs of a normal delivery. The insurance benefits on a normal delivery usually are about ten times the amount the policy allows per day for hospital room and board charges.

SAVINGS: "Next to how much you make, the most important thing in money management is how much you save," says Mrs. Marion Stevens Eberly of the Institute of Life Insurance. "This is because unless you can satisfy yourself that you are saving what you should, nothing else in your spending and saving plan will give you any peace. You will be back where you started, worrying whether you can afford this or afford that every time you buy anything at all.

"A good rule is to always save for something. If you know you are saving for a new car or for Christmas presents or for your family's future security, you can be as sensible about saving as you are about buying things. You will know what your savings goals are and will be able to proceed accordingly, without vague worries whether you are saving too much or not enough.

"It is particularly important to know your goals when you save for your family's future security or for your retirement. You can take a sheet of paper and list property, life insurance, bank accounts and the other things you own. Underneath, you can then write down what these mean in terms of security for your family."

What should your savings objective be? Most authorities agree that you should aim to keep about six months of your income in a savings account, where it will draw safe dividends and work for you. If you wish to accumulate this reserve in five years' time—a reasonable objective—you should save about 10 percent of your salary every pay day.

AUTOMOBILE: The average family tends to underestimate car expenses. "You should consider both fixed and flexible expenses," says Miss Heuer. "Fixed expenses occur at regular intervals and include:

"Installment payments (principal and interest) if you finance the car; insurance; city and state license fees on your car and costs for driver's licenses; garage rent if you rent a garage.

"Flexible expenses include costs that occur irregularly and in varying amounts. These include:

"Gasoline costs. You can determine the cost per mile by dividing the number of miles your car runs per gallon into the cost per gallon. To be sure of accuracy, take your mileage estimate over a long period of normal driving.

"Oil costs. These average about .1 cent per mile.

"Tire costs. Figure about .4 cents per mile for light cars, .5 cents for heavy ones.

"Maintenance costs. For greasing, washing, and regular inspection and servicing costs, estimate .8 cents per mile for a low-priced car, .9 cents for a heavier, higher-priced one.

"Miscellaneous expenses. Costs for polishing, parking, inspection, tolls, anti-freeze, and other maintenance average about .1 cent per mile."

In addition to these basic major expenses, you will have to allow certain amounts each month for personal items: meals for the husband if he works away from home, cigarettes, haircuts, beauty treatments and so on. A sum should be set aside for furniture and household equipment (appliances such as television set, clothes-washer, etc.) for the purchase and repair of clothing, for contributions to church and charities, for entertainment and education.

Of course, your spending plan will depend upon your income and the number of your dependents, among other factors. Your particular circumstances probably differ in some ways from the average.

One husband lives within walking distance of work and

returns home for lunch, so his transportation and lunch expenses are much lower than usual. His family can make a different use of the money generally allocated for that purpose. Another man is a host at an expensive restaurant, and must be perfectly groomed at all times. Obviously, his clothing expenses will be higher than average and his family must cut expenses elsewhere so that he can maintain his wardrobe. Another family lives where apartments are scarce and their outlay for rent is excessive. They must save on entertainment to make up for it.

Regardless of the plan you adopt, only a small part of your income probably will be devoted to basic absolute necessities—food, shelter, etc. The rest will be used for things you could do without at no sacrifice to health—entertainment, automobiles, beauty treatments, vacations, tobacco, alcohol. Of course, even persons earning low salaries can have many of those non-essentials and yet live within their income. When families get into financial hot water, it is generally because they have spent more on non-essentials than they should have.

The important point to remember is that you can plan your expenses intelligently—if you want to. Once you begin to do so, you take the most important step towards financial stability, towards the enjoyment of more carefree living, towards security for your family when your children are growing, and for your own old age when you can no longer earn an income.

Seven Steps to a Good Spending Plan

Here are suggestions by Helen White, executive secretary of the National Thrift Committee, to help you prepare your spending plan:

- *Keep it realistic.* Base it on what you know from experience of your ordinary and extraordinary expenses. Use cancelled checks and receipts to help you to determine where

To Live Better, You Need a Spending Plan

SOME SUGGESTED SPENDING PLANS

Monthly Income After Taxes	No. in Family	Savings	Food	Shelter	Clothing	Operating	Advancement & Entertainment
200	2	$15	$70	$45	$18	$18	$34
200	4	7	85	45	20	20	23
250	2	30	75	50	23	20	52
250	4	20	95	50	25	22	38
300	2	40	79	65	30	25	61
300	4	25	103	65	35	27	45
350	2	50	87	70	35	32	76
350	4	35	105	70	45	35	60
400	2	65	97	80	40	38	80
400	4	50	120	80	48	39	65
450	2	90	103	85	45	40	87
450	4	75	124	85	54	42	70
500	2	100	115	90	55	45	95
500	4	90	135	90	65	45	75
600	2	120	125	110	60	55	130
600	4	95	145	110	75	55	120
700	2	165	130	125	65	65	150
700	4	115	165	125	85	70	140
800	2	155	145	140	80	75	175
800	4	135	175	140	100	75	175
900	2	220	160	150	90	85	195
900	4	150	205	150	115	85	195
1000	2	250	190	165	110	85	200
1000	4	170	245	165	130	90	200
Your Estimate							

—Source: The American Bankers Association

These figures are merely suggestions to help you develop a monthly savings and spending plan in line with your own family's needs and interests. One family will desire to spend more on food, another may prefer to spend more on clothing. For this reason, you should prepare your own budget and not rely upon those, such as the above, which are based on averages for the entire country. In the above plan, "Savings" includes not only savings accounts but equity in insurance, pension plans, stocks and bonds, etc.

and how you spent your money. Your new plan should conform closely to known, fixed expenses—rent, utility bills and insurance payments.

If you have just been married, wait a month or so before you try to set up a plan. Then you will know, in general, what your spending patterns are.

• *Keep it simple.* Don't get into a job of detailed bookkeeping, trying to keep track of every penny you use. But keep accurate records so that you can tell generally (if not with absolute precision) whether your money is going where you want it to go.

• *Develop new patterns gradually.* If you have been spending inordinate amounts on entertainment, do not cut it out entirely. Merely cut down. A budget may be hard to live with if it suddenly denies you pleasures you are used to. Moreover, you won't be able to change long-established habits over night.

• *Provide allowances for everyone in the family.* Some budgets go haywire because husbands and wives both dig into one sum set aside for personal allowances. Neither feels fully responsible for seeing that no more than the stipulated amount is spent. Husband, wife and children should have certain amounts they can spend as they please.

• *Make each partner responsible for several expense departments.* The husband might pay housing expenses, utility bills, automobile expenses, and major entertainment items. The wife might pay for food, household furnishings, clothing, laundry, and other household expenses. Each partner is then responsible for keeping within the allotted amounts.

• *Be willing to change your plan if necessary.* It should serve you—you should not be its slave. It should help you get more of what you want from life. If it fails, something is wrong with the budget or your approach to it. If it seems too strict to live with, hold another family discussion and change it. If you fail at several attempts to set up a workable spending plan, your own attitudes may require changing. For no one can indefinitely spend more than he makes. At some point, we must all learn to be satisfied with what we can afford.

• *Know how to make the plan work.* If you budget a lower amount for an item than you usually spend, decide how you will achieve the economy. A couple had regularly spent $40 a month to run their automobile—for gas, oil, grease jobs, motor repairs. They decided to cut the outlay to $25. To make their plan work, they agreed to these specific steps:

To deal with a station giving a discount of two cents a gallon.

To avoid needless driving and to use the car only when they would perform two or more errands.

To buy oil in bulk and fill the crankcase themselves, instead of paying more than twice as much for it at gas stations.

To shop at discount houses for standard-brand tires, batteries and other equipment.

They succeeded in reducing their expenditures according to plan, but only because they knew how to make their wishes come true.

How to Make Your Spending Plan Work

You can use several different mechanical devices to help you stick to your budget. Here is a common one:

Each pay period, put into different envelopes the specific sums you plan to spend on different categories—food, clothing, rent, utility bills, insurance, etc. You probably will not need more than eight or ten envelopes. Try to avoid borrowing from one fund to meet deficits in another. If you spend more than you should on food during one period, and are running low on funds in that category, cut your food expenditures at once. Use food on hand—canned goods, staples, etc.—to prepare meals. If necessary, go on a Spartan diet until the next pay period.

Some families put a certain amount in a "miscellaneous" envelope each month and use it as a kind of lending agency.

For example, if the amount in the utilities envelope cannot cover an unusually large telephone bill, the amount is taken from the miscellaneous envelope. But the next pay period, the sum is paid back to "miscellaneous" out of the allowance for utilities, and the family tries to keep phone bills down until the balance in the utilities envelope is back to normal.

By keeping separate allowances in separate envelopes, you can maintain a constant check on how well you are staying within the limits you have set. Of course, if you run short month after month in any category, you should either curb your spending or revise your plan to make it more realistic.

chapter two

HOW TO GET THE MOST FOR YOUR MONEY WHEN YOU SHOP

Apply these suggestions and every eighty cents you spend can do the work of a dollar.

You can acquire a skill as a money manager which will pay dividends every day of your life. It will enable you consistently to put your shopping dollars to the most effective use, to buy the best quality merchandise at the lowest prices, to obtain for $7 or $8 the things for which your neighbors pay $10.

There are many aspects to the art of shopping and many fine points to be mastered. But here is the essence of what you should know—the fundamental rules, based on the experience of home economists, merchants, oficials of government agencies, managers of Better Business Bureaus.

Don't Buy on Impulse

If you observe this four-word principle, you can save up to 25 percent in your day-in, day-out shopping, many authorities told me.

Most of us do not realize how much we spend on things we had no intention of getting when we left our homes. The packaging industry has grown to greatness by making products so attractive that we want them as soon as we see them. Tens of millions of dollars are spent each year on posters to catch our interest—and cash—at "points of purchase." Each year we spend hundreds of millions after high-pressure sales talks which we had no thought of falling for when we left home.

If we shop with a child in a food supermarket, we probably will reach the check-out counter with candy, cookies, cake or ice cream we originally did not plan to purchase. In the department store, we are attracted by bargains—"too good to resist," although we do not need what we buy. We start out for bread and milk at the delicatessen, but the fragrance of other foods proves overwhelming. We leave with exotic—and expensive—delicacies. When we enter a clothing store, we can afford only a certain price for a dress or suit, but we let the sales clerk "upgrade" us and talk us into something more expensive.

Many persons condone impulse-buying because "it's fun." Few families want to live on a budget without room for optional purchases, and most can buy on impulse occasionally without hurting themselves financially. But those who habitually indulge in spur-of-the-moment whims almost inevitably will soon lack money for more important purposes. In fact, most families' financial troubles stem from this inability to curb impulse-spending.

How can you put firm controls over this kind of buying? Here are three suggestions by economists:

Before you leave home on a shopping expedition, list the things you intend to buy. Do not buy other items unless you will need them within the next few days, and you have forgotten to include them in your list—items like bread, soap and butter.

Before leaving home, also decide how much you will spend at each shop for each particular purpose—so much for groceries, so much for shoes, etc. These figures should be based upon past experience and should be realistic. Do not exceed them for any reason.

How to Get the Most for Your Money When You Shop 15

If you spot a bargain sale of something you have not planned to buy, resist the impulse, no matter how low the price. Go home and consider the matter calmly. In most cases, you will have plenty of time to take advantage of the sale *if* you finally decide to buy the "bargain."

Double-Check Major Purchases

Many corporations require a top executive to approve a purchase order for goods or services exceeding a certain amount —perhaps $100. Since he often has a different viewpoint from the one doing the buying, this rule makes it more likely that the firm's money will be well-spent.

Many experts have told me that families can use this method to good effect. A husband and wife decided that neither would spend more than $50 at any time without consulting the other. Before, they had been impulse-spenders. A camera enthusiast, he had frequently bought equipment which he used a few times and then discarded. She found it difficult to resist bargain-priced dresses which she never wore as frequently as she had expected. Once this couple began to double-check, however, their purchases of items over $50 dropped sharply, but their living standards remained virtually unaffected. They built a respectable bank balance for the first time. And their major purchases were made with intelligence, not emotions.

Comparison Shop on Major Items

Another procedure of corporations can make your own shopping more effective:

Never buy any item over a certain amount unless you first get prices from three stores. Obviously, "comparison shopping" is undesirable when small amounts are involved. But on major items, those costing $25 or more, for instance, it can be a big money-saver.

Comparison-shoppers frequently find almost unbelievable differences in prices. One store has excellent values in clothing, but prices household appliances at, or close to, the manufacturers' list prices. A competitive store offers inferior clothing at high cost, but offers big savings in its appliance department.

Buy for Cash and Forego Unnecessary Services

If you use a charge account, if you shop where a sales clerk always stands ready to help you, and if you wish to have even small parcels delivered, you must be prepared to pay. True, such services virtually guarantee consumer satisfaction and often save much time, but a store which caters to customers in this way obviously has more expenses than one which has eliminated unnecessary services.

Experts have told me that shopping at a typical cash-and-carry, self-service store should result in average savings of from 15 to 25 percent. For example, cash-and-carry discount houses, which have sprung up all over the country, usually sell household appliances at prices 20 to 40 percent below manufacturers' list prices. At these places, however, you may face some inconveniences and hazards. For instance:

• *You must be prepared for indifferent, and frequently insolent, service.* To keep overhead down, these stores deliberately keep their sales help to a minimum. You may have to examine the merchandise and get all the facts about it yourself, then search out a clerk to handle your order.

• *You may get stuck on "blind merchandise."* You can verify prices on established trade name brands with established list prices. But on merchandise with little-known brand names —items like bedding, sheets and linens—it may be difficult for you to find out what the original price was really meant to be. This is a real hazard with furniture. The National Better Business Bureau has often warned that dealers cannot possibly consistently sell it at "wholesale prices."

- *You may have few or no return privileges.* Most established discount houses will refund your money if you return unused merchandise within a few days, but they may refuse to take it back if you have used it even slightly or lack sales slips to prove that you did not buy it elsewhere.
- *You may have a very limited variety of goods to choose from.* Discount stores often refuse to carry goods they cannot sell profitably at substantial discounts. Unlike department stores, they feel no obligation to stock items solely as a convenience for customers. When shopping for major appliances particularly, you may find your choice restricted to a few models the dealer has space to display.
- *You may be unable to buy on credit.* Some discount houses will arrange credit terms with local banks if you wish to charge your purchases. But their interest rates often greatly exceed those at department stores. If you buy discount house products on the installment plan, you may have to make your own credit arrangements outside to effect any over-all savings.

Wait for Special Sales

Many stores regularly announce sales of various kinds at which genuine bargains are available.

"Clearance Sales" usually offer the largest price cuts. These may also be advertised as close-out sales, end-of-season sales, inventory sales and sample sales. They consist of stocks, generally left at the end of a selling season, which the store wishes to dispose of to make way for new merchandise. For instance, in July you can expect lower prices on summer furniture, bathing suits, light-weight suits and dresses. In February, overcoats and winter wear will be marked down.

Prices at clearance sales are sometimes 50 percent below those at the height of the selling season. But your choice may be limited. The store offers only goods which customers examined at regular prices and passed up.

"Special Purchase Sales" frequently provide spectacular opportunities. Perhaps the Spring is cold and wet and a lawn mower factory is stocked with machines. The manufacturer may offer them to retailers at prices considerably below his usual ones in order to avoid having capital tied up all year. Perhaps a merchant goes out of business and sells his stock to a going concern. Or a manufacturer of television sets plans to introduce a new model, but first wishes to dispose of his old sets. These typical conditions all set the stage for special-purchase sales.

Some merchants have regular arrangements to buy merchandise which does not meet a manufacturer's standards of quality. This merchandise may be called "irregulars" if its imperfections can barely be seen and will not affect wearing qualities, or "seconds" if the imperfections are more obvious. A store which runs one sale on "irregulars" or "seconds" will usually do so again. If you call its buyer, you may even be told when to expect a sale.

"Annual Sales" and "annual events" consist of a store's regular goods especially marked down for the occasion. After the sale, the unsold merchandise is generally offered again at its regular price.

Many stores hold sales on white goods, towels, blankets, resort wear and furs in January; on china, glassware, rugs, furniture and housewares in February and August or September; on housewares, china and silver, hosiery, shoes and men's and boys' clothing in March; on spring-cleaning supplies, lingerie and underwear in April; on air conditioners and fans in May; on all kinds of clothing in August. At these sales you might buy merchandise at 15 or 20 percent below their regular price. Wise shoppers often wait for them, then buy enough to last them until the next event can be expected.

Learn to Interpret Advertisements

"Only suckers pay list prices," the average American believes. Increasing numbers regularly use this principle in buying everything from automobiles to xylophones. Many first consider the list price of an item, then ask how great a reduction is offered; a price slash of less than 30 percent is not a true "bargain."

In Oscar Wilde's famous phrase, such people know "the price of everything and the value of nothing." Some merchants have become aware of this fact. When they advertise, they keep their selling prices substantially below some other price —a list price, comparable retail price, original price—that is often far removed from reality. The use of deceptive prices has created what Victor H. Nyborg, president of the Association of Better Business Bureaus, has termed one of the greatest problems for the American consumer.

Even reputable stores sometimes use ads that are partially deceptive. An alert consumer, by refusing to take commonly used advertising phrases at face value, can often determine when a bargain is really a bargain—or when she would probably waste her time in looking at the merchandise.

Here are phrases often used in store ads, and what they might actually mean:

"40 Percent Off List Price." This might be the manufacturer's list price, and perhaps it was originally intended that the merchandise be sold for this price. Sometimes, however, manufacturers inflate list prices so that any dealer might sell at a "discount" and still make a normal profit. Some even place ads in national publications emphasizing the inflated prices. Merchants display the ad to "prove" that they are selling the goods far below "list price." Their selling price often is the real list price.

"Regular $59.95 Value." This phrase is meaningless because

it does not specifically tell you what the item regularly sells for. Another store may offer it regularly at prices as low as or even lower than the one now advertised. Similar phrases which say nothing: "Comparable value," "Usual $59.95 value," "Comparable list price."

"Made to sell for $19.95." No law prevents a manufacturer from making a ten cent item to sell for $100. The question is: Was the expected selling price a reasonable one to expect? Since the goods are now offered for much less, the price probably was inflated at the start.

"Originally." This phrase is often abused by clothing stores. A national men's store priced a wool suit at $79.95. At the end of the season, it offered the suit at a clearance sale for $49.95, failed to sell it, then marked it down to $39 in a "final clearance." Still unsold, the suit was passed on to a bargain clothing chain which offered it at $29.50. By now, however, the wool in the garment had lost some elasticity with age and the style was somewhat out of date. If the buyer had been told when the suit was $79.95, he might have surmised those facts. It was no bargain at the price he paid.

Some ads say something like: "Last week we sold the identical article for $39. Special today, $29." Here you may have a bargain—if the store is trustworthy.

"Below manufacturers' cost to make," and "below usual wholesale cost." These claims may be true in some cases—for example, where manufacturers misjudge demands, make more than they can sell, and must unload their goods to get cash. But these instances are rare. Goods sold at a price lower than the cost to make are likely to be inferior, since the maker could not sell them at regular prices.

Officials of Better Business Bureaus state that you should be suspicious if merchandise is advertised at more than 50 percent below regular or list prices. Most stores try to make a profit of around 40 percent, and while they may occasionally sell goods at a loss, they obviously cannot remain in business if they do so consistently. If merchandise is marked down more than 50 percent, look for these possible reasons:

• *The item on sale is either an "irregular" or a "second."* If so, it would not be sold at regular list prices anyway.

• *It is a demonstration or floor model.* A television set which has been switched on and off thousands of times is not worth as much as one in a sealed carton. Appliances, dishwashers, clothes-washers, etc. may be scratched or nicked.

• *It is a discontinued model.* A store advertised 60 percent off on tape-recorders. Readers needed perfect vision to see the letters "disc." in the advertisement, an admission that the model had been discontinued. When buyers had to make repairs later, spare parts were not available.

• *It is an out-moded style.* This is a strong possibility in the case of clothing. It may be shop-worn. Colors may be faded. Fabrics may lack resiliency.

• *The merchandise is "distress" goods.* It may have been purchased from a salvage company as a result of a fire or bankruptcy.

If none of these conditions exist, and the store fails to explain convincingly why it can sell at prices below normal wholesale costs, you can reasonably suspect that there is something false about the "list price," "original price," or other price used as a basis of comparison.

Be a Label Reader

Government agencies require manufacturers and processors of food, drugs, clothing, furniture and other products to indicate their contents on the label. You can often learn more from these labels than from wordy advertisements. For example, many items in your medicine cabinet must conform to government formulas, and any product which meets U. S. Pharmacopoeia ("U.S.P.") standards is safe, regardless of brand. Thus 100 tablets of U.S.P. aspirin sold under a store's private label for nineteen cents may be a better buy than the same quantity of another brand sold for 59¢.

According to law, all vitamin preparations must clearly show the strength of their ingredients on the label. If you compare two products containing vitamins of the same potency, you may find one priced 40 to 50 percent below the other.

Canned fruits and vegetables often are graded "A," "B" and "C," according to their quality and appearance. When the grade of the contents is disclosed on the label, you have an excellent way of determining the respective values of different brands. Checking of labels also will help you save greatly in buying meats.

Knowing what the product is made of is even more important when you buy "blind items" where lack of a manufacturer's name you know may give you a sense of insecurity. Only by reading labels, for example, can you be sure that cotton goods are Sanforized and can be washed without shrinking. A label will tell you whether a shirt will recover its shape after washing or will require pressing every time.

Master These Tricks of Supermarket Shopping

One of the few benefits of the depression of the 1930s was that it spurred the development of food supermarkets. This self-service idea, now firmly entrenched, enables you to save 20 percent or more on your food bills.

By bringing all the food a family needs under one roof, supermarkets are also invaluable time-savers. Visit a European market, where housewives trudge from store to store to obtain different foods, and you can quickly accept supermarket owners' claims that the savings in time this system makes possible are even greater than those in money.

Supermarkets cut all the costs which add to the price of your food. They buy in huge quantities and can often get carload-lot prices. They maintain a low ratio of employee to customer, since you do the work of selecting your purchases. They eliminate delivery charges, because you carry your purchase to your home yourself. They have no expensive credit operations, since they usually operate on a cash-only basis. They also have extremely low margins of profit. The Supermarket Institute states that the net profit of large food chains generally amounts to little more than a penny on every dollar of food sold.

While supermarket shopping will almost certainly cut your food costs, you can use many tricks to get even greater values. Here are tested ones:

• *Habitually read the food pages of your newspaper.* Watch particularly for the week-end specials generally advertised on Thursdays. Stories and ads in your newspaper will tell you what meats, fruits and vegetables are low-priced and in season. Plan your meals around these bargains. Since budget favorites vary from month to month, there is little danger that you will tire of the meats and vegetables which are plentiful at any moment.

• *Make out a complete shopping list.* Include all items on sale and all staples you will need for the week or longer. If a staple is offered at an exceptionally low price, make a note to buy a large quantity. Some stores sell at lower prices if you buy by the case. You will save much time if you list together all the items found near each other in the store—canned goods together, dairy product together, etc.

• *Guard against impulse buying.* A report by Sales Management Magazine says that when Mother shops alone, she generally follows her list carefully to keep within her budget. When Dad shops with her, he chooses more expensive meats and tosses snack materials and other foods into the shopping cart. When the whole family is there, the shopping trip becomes a holiday project and the bill is much higher than it would be otherwise.

• *Look for private grocery brands.* The store may put its

own label on products processed by the manufacturers of nationally-advertised brands. They are often as good as the known brands but may be priced 15 to 20 percent lower. You can find private brands in baked goods and bread, canned fruits and vegetables, frozen foods, flour, dairy products, coffee and tea.

• *Buy economy sizes and quantities.* Large cans of fruit and vegetables may cost 25 percent less per ounce than smaller sizes. If your family can use large sizes without wastage, get them by all means. But, warns the Institute of Home Economics of the U. S. Department of Agriculture, "a big, economy-size package or a large quantity of a food especially priced is no bargain if you tire of it and it grows stale or spoils."

• *Remember the use you intend to make of the food.* When used for cooking, lower priced canned tomatoes serve as well as more expensive ones. Their appearance, which is largely responsible for their price, is not a factor in this case. You can substitute brown "B" eggs for white "A" ones in baking without endangering the flavor. Where recipes call for whole milk, you can use dry powdered milk at less than half the cost.

• *Remember that you pay for the convenience of packaged foods.* Here are examples by A. A. Irwin, produce director of Operation, Inc., of New York:

"The ton value at retail of the most popular cake mixes varies from $500 to over $1,100. But family flour in 25-pound bags retails at about $150 a ton.

"A 10-pound bag of potatoes retails at 39¢—or $78 per ton. Potatoes washed, cleaned and wrapped in aluminum foil retail for 29¢—about $257 per ton. A 12-ounce package of peeled potatoes, cut for French frying, retails at 19¢—about $506 per ton."

• *Learn to judge quality in meats.* A survey for the Supermarket Institute revealed that women shoppers often buy the most expensive cuts simply because they do not know how to compare values or to prepare low-cost meats properly. Since meat is the most costly item in the food budget, you will be equipped to save much money if you learn how to identify federal grades of meat as established by the U. S. Department of Agriculture:

BEEF: Six official grades of beef may be found in retail stores. Look on the side of the meat for the official stamping. It is done with a harmless purple vegetable juice which usually disappears in cooking.

"Prime," the top quality, comes from young, well-fed beef-type cattle. It has liberal "marbling," quantities of fat within the lean, and is juicy, tender and flavorful. Most prime grade beef is sold to restaurants.

"Choice" is high quality but usually has less fat than Prime. Roasts and steaks from the loin and rib are tender and juicy. Cuts from the round or chuck are more suitable for braising and pot-roasting, but should be tender with a well-developed flavor.

"Good" has little fat but is of fairly good quality. Cuts lack the juiciness of higher grades but are sometimes preferred for their relative tenderness and high proportion of lean.

"Standard" has but a thin covering of fat. It is mild in flavor and usually is relatively tender when properly prepared.

"Commercial" comes from older cattle and usually lacks the tenderness of the higher grades. Most cuts require long slow cooking with moist heat to make them tender and to develop the full beef flavor.

"Utility" is produced mostly from the oldest cattle and usually lacks natural tenderness and juiciness. Cuts have little fat but provide a palatable meat for pot-roasting, stewing, boiling or ground-meat dishes. For best results, slow cooking by moist heat is essential.

LAMB, YEARLING MUTTON, MUTTON. Meat from sheep is divided into three classes according to its age when slaughtered—lamb, yearling mutton, and mutton. Official grades for lamb and yearling mutton are USDA Prime, Choice, Good, Utility, and Cull. Official grades for mutton are USDA Choice, Good, Utility, and Cull.

Lamb meat is usually light red, and fine in texture. Since lamb is from young animals, most cuts are sufficiently tender to be cooked by dry heat. Roasting, broiling, and pan-broiling are the usual methods of cooking.

Typical mutton is dark red. It is from mature animals and may lack natural tenderness. Braising or pot-roasting is generally used to develop tenderness and flavor. Higher grades of both lamb and mutton should be more tender and juicy, with less bone than lower grades.

VEAL AND CALF. Official grades are USDA, Prime, Choice, Good, Standard, Utility, and Cull.

Typical veal is from animals 3 months old or younger which have subsisted largely on milk. The lean meat is grayish pink. Higher grades are more thickly fleshed and have more fat than the lower grades and thus are more juicy and flavorful. Moist heat methods are needed to insure juiciness and development of flavor.

Typical calf is from animals between 3 and 8 months old which have had foods other than milk for a long time. Calf is between veal and beef in color, texture, flavor, tenderness, and juiciness.

When comparing prices of meat and other foods, says the Institute of Home Economics of the U. S. Department of Agriculture, "figure cost per serving rather than what you pay for a pound. For example, if meat has much gristle or bone, one usual size serving may take half a pound, or even a pound. At the other extreme, if there is no bone, a pound makes four or five servings of average size."

If you are permitted to do so, select your own fruits and vegetables for the purposes you have in mind, for what may be best for one use will be poor for another. Other suggestions, by Gerald R. Blount of the U. S. Department of Agriculture:

"Remember that the largest is not always the best nor the most economical . . . Avoid commodities that show decay, particularly if you do not intend to use them at once. Slightly decayed stock bought at a low price may not be cheap if the waste offsets the reduction in price . . . Do not buy merely because prices are low. But if they are low because the commodity is over-abundant, you may be getting a bargain . . . When fruits and vegetables that are locally grown are in season, there is generally an abundant supply at low prices. A knowledge of local conditions will help you to estimate market prices and is useful if you plan to can or preserve certain commodities . . . See that containers hold full measure, and have not been packed so that the best specimens are on top with poor stock beneath . . . Distinguish between blemishes that affect appearance and those that affect eating quality. Sooty, blotched or fly-specked apples, dirty potatoes or those with growth cracks, and cabbage with spotted or yellowed outer leaves are examples of other excellent produce with surface blemishes which can usually be removed."

Adds R. A. Seelig, director of information of the United Fresh Fruit and Vegetable Association:

"Many fruits, including apricots, apples early in the season, avocados, cantaloupes and other musk-melons, mangoes, peaches, persimmons, pineapples, plums and prunes often or usually are purchased not fully ripe. Bananas also often are purchased somewhat green. The same is true of tomatoes. Such fruits need to be held at room temperature to bring them to the desired stage of juiciness and ripeness, but don't over-do it. After ripening, refrigerate.

"Apricots can be held until they soften; apples until they yield slightly to gentle pressure (but the best test is to bite into one); avocados until soft; pears until they are perfumey and yellow, if Bartletts, or fragrant, but still green, if Anjous;

cantaloupes until fragrant and springy under gentle pressure; mangoes until soft and fragrant; peaches until juicy; persimmons until jelly-like in consistency; pineapples until fragrant and the spikes pull out easily; plums and prunes until soft; bananas until all yellow or until all but the tip is yellow; tomatoes until well reddened.

"As to vegetables, no maturing period is required. They are ready to eat. Most vegetables (but not potatoes, sweet-potatoes or dry onions) should be refrigerated. To preserve quality, prevent them from drying out. This can be done by placing them in film bags or hydrators in the refrigerator. Green, leafy and yellow vegetables can be sprinkled before putting them away. This helps to conserve their own moisture."

Learn to Detect Gyps

Most businessmen realize that they must give fair value if they expect to build a list of regular customers. They believe, as the slogan puts it, that "a satisfied customer is their best advertisement." But the public must also beware of gyp operators who flourish everywhere and take millions of dollars from unsuspecting consumers every year.

Better Business Bureaus do an outstanding job of exposing crooked business practices wherever they appear. They have alerted the public to hundreds of flagrant schemes and have put thousands of rackets out of operation. But as soon as one racket is exposed, another becomes widespread. Often consumers who see through the first gyp are bilked by the second.

This happens because the average person does not realize that most rackets have basic characteristics in common. If you can recognize these characteristics, you will be able to protect yourself against *all* illegitimate schemes—whether it is a spectacular "going-out-of-business" sale, a home improvement job, a "bargain" offer made over radio or television, or any other proposition that is certain to leave you dissatisfied. Here is how to avoid losing your money to swindlers who pose as businessmen:

• *Never expect something for nothing.* Managers of Better Business Bureaus throughout the U. S. (and Canada) told me that most illegitimate offers appeal to a basic human instinct to obtain things of value without paying for them. Of course, no merchant can stay in business by selling merchandise at a loss or by giving it away. Yet many operators exploit the unwillingness of people to believe this. For instance:

A dance studio ran childishly simple crossword puzzles in newspaper ads and announced that anyone who solved the puzzles correctly would receive lessons worth $25. Those who rose to the bait got a "prize" worth less than $1. The dance studio then used high pressure to sell them a series of lessons costing hundreds of dollars.

A home improvement contractor promised to install new roofing for fantastically low prices if homeowners would let him show his work to other prospects. He told them they would get $50 for each sale that resulted. Of course, they would have to pay the full price—a high one. Visualizing hundreds of dollars in commissions, many agreed to the deal. They found themselves with shoddy installations and collected no commissions.

Newspaper ads offered complete furnace installations for $325—less than half the usual price. Bargain-hunters received undersized furnaces and poorly-installed heating systems. The inefficient heating plant raised their fuel bills much higher than the average for homes of similar size.

• *Beware of door-bell salesmen.* Many legitimate companies sell merchandise this way and will give you satisfaction if you complain about anything you buy. But files of Better Business Bureaus also testify that a high percentage of frauds start at the front door.

The door-to-door salesman may represent that he is a "government inspector," that he is in a contest to send poor children to camp, or that he is engaged in some other idealistic enterprise. His aim is to lower your guard so that you will be more receptive to what he has to sell.

A man rang a door bell in a Boston suburb. When a young mother answered, he said he was an inspector sent to investigate her furnace. After a few minutes, the man emerged from the cellar, said that the joints would require cementing immediately, wrote something on a blank and told her to sign. Without realizing that she was authorizing him to repair the furnace, she did so. The next day, three mechanics began working on the furnace. At the end of the day, they presented her with a bill for $150, which she legally had to pay.

If a door-to-door salesman represents a company or product you know and his prices appear reasonable, you might be justified in dealing with him. But a combination of door-to-door salesmanship and a promise of a substantial gift for nothing is an almost certain invitation to financial loss.

• *Think twice before you sign anything.* Many rackets consist in getting a customer to sign a contract while keeping him from realizing what he is doing. Once you sign, you cannot change your mind and are legally obliged to go through with the deal. Your signature usually makes a contract, and contracts that turn sour are the greatest cause of trouble that reaches to Better Business Bureaus or the civil courts.

"Buyers often make contracts without realizing it, or fail to protect themselves with a contract when they should," says Aubra Johnston, manager of the Chicago Better Business Bureau. Here are some frequent mistakes:

"I didn't know I had signed a contract; the paper didn't say it was." One man ordered a porch built, and signed a simple paragraph agreeing to pay $600. After waiting two weeks, he changed his mind. When the contractor delivered the material and started to work, the customer told him to cancel the job. The contractor insisted that the buyer had to pay, for it is a fact that agreements need not be labeled as contracts to be valid.

"I signed a contract on Sunday, thinking it was not binding." A contract made on Sundays or holidays *is* valid. "A storm window salesman called on me one Sunday morning," a woman complained. "He talked for two hours. I wanted to get rid of him to go to church, so I signed. I don't want the windows." But she had to take them—and pay.

"I signed a contract with a guarantee. Now I want my money back." A "guarantee" is meaningless unless the contract spells out exactly what is guaranteed, and what recourse the buyer has. It is of extreme importance to know and understand the limitations and terms of guarantee. Some are full of loopholes. For example, fly-by-night painters advertised that they would paint a house with a new mastic "guaranteed for ten years." Victims signed a contract which reads "Guarantee: This work is *registered* for ten years." Often within a few months, the paint began to peel. Homeowners who tried to have their money refunded discovered that the "guarantee" meant nothing.

"I never got a copy of the contract I signed." Buyers are entitled to one. But if you do not get one, you still have made a valid contract.

"I didn't read what I signed, therefore the contract is not valid." This is a common fallacy. For your signature says in effect that you knew what you were doing.

- *Beware of bait advertising.* "To attract new customers," an appliance store advertised television sets with a 17-inch screen for $79.95. A young husband and wife sped to the store when the ad appeared, and asked a salesman to show them the set. He shook his head and said the last one had just been sold.

"But I have another model with features the one on sale didn't have," he said. He then high-pressured the couple into buying a set costing $50 more than the one they had planned to get.

This was an example of "bait advertising" at its worst—a practice which has also become widespread in recent years. Robert M. Parrish, executive director of the Federal Trade Commission, defines bait advertising as "an alluring but insincere offer to sell a product or service which the advertiser in truth does not intend or want to sell. Its purpose is to switch consumers from buying the advertised merchandise, in order to sell something else, usually at a higher price or on a basis more advantageous to the advertiser. The primary aim of a bait advertisement is to obtain leads as to persons interested in buying merchandise of the type so advertised."

How can you tell when you have been "baited"? Mr. Parrish says these are typical signs of an unscrupulous merchant:

"Refusal to show, demonstrate, or sell the product offered in accordance with the terms of the offer;

"Disparagement by acts or words of the advertised product or of the guarantee, credit terms, availability of service, repairs or parts, or in any other respect, in connection with it;

"Failure to have available at all outlets listed in the advertisement a sufficient quantity of the advertised product to meet reasonably anticipated demands, unless the advertisement clearly and adequately discloses that supply is limited and/or the merchandise is available only at designated outlets;

"Refusal to take orders for the advertised merchandise to be delivered within a reasonable period of time;

"Showing or demonstrating of a product which is defective, unusable or impractical for the purpose represented or implied in the advertisement;

"Use of a sales plan or method of compensation for salesmen or penalizing salesmen, designed to prevent or discourage them from selling the advertised product."

Bait ads are often used by dealers who will send salesmen to your home. You see storm windows advertised at $9.95 and ask to have a salesman display them to you. He insists that you would be ashamed to have such inferior windows but that his $19.95 units are ideal for your purpose. Such tactics are ample evidence that neither the salesman nor the company he represents can be trusted.

When reputable stores have only limited quantities of merchandise on sale and expect an early sell-out, they usually warn you in advance. If you arrive too late, they generally do not try to thrust something more expensive on you. According to Better Business Bureaus, when a salesman under such circumstances is determined to sell something higher-priced, you can be fairly sure that you have been "baited." To protect your own interests, leave the store at once, and give your business to other places thereafter.

chapter three

THE TWO EDGES OF CREDIT

It is a great help when you use it properly, but it can ruin you if you don't. Here is how to tell the difference

Not so long ago, many men went through life boasting that they "never owed a cent." They paid cash for everything they bought. They thought it was a sign of weak character if a family mortgaged its home. They lived by the slogan of old New England: "Pay as you go—or stay home."

Few persons could make such a boast today. We live in an Age of Credit. Rare is the home *without* a mortgage. Rare is the family without a charge account, rare the couple who have not bought an appliance on the installment plan, rare the businessman who does not carry a credit card.

We are so accustomed to credit that the person who has never used it may sometimes be at a disadvantage. Consider the tale of a 45-year old man, reared in the "pay as you go" tradition, who paid cash for everything. His wife bought her groceries at a supermarket and her clothing at a store that sold only for cash. Then she became seriously ill. As usual, the doctor's bills were staggering. The man dug into their savings account to pay them, and when he reached bottom he applied to a commercial bank for a personal loan. The bank's loan officer examined him suspiciously. "I'm sorry," he said, "but it seems peculiar that a man your age has no credit record. Are you sure you haven't changed your name—that you're not trying to hide something?" It was weeks before the man obtained his loan. Meanwhile, other applicants, less conscientious about their financial obligations, received theirs within days through the bank's "push button" credit system.

Almost everyone recognizes that credit, wisely used, can be beneficial. It can greatly aid you to achieve a happy life. It can help you to reach a higher standard of living than has ever been possible anywhere.

Credit has made Americans the world's greatest nation of homeowners. You need only a small down payment and a steady income to buy one. Thanks to liberal credit terms, you can pay off your mortgage like rent; after a period of years, you will own your home free and clear. In earlier days, couples often waited until they saved the entire price before they bought a house, by which time their children were too old to benefit from it. Or else they paid rent all their lives.

Credit has put the nation on wheels, has made us the most travelling people on earth. Most new automobiles on American roads are sold on the installment plan.

Credit enables families with modest incomes to educate their children in college. Long-term loans, which the student himself can help to pay back, are making the opportunities of higher education available to almost everyone with ability.

Credit is like many other things in life—fine in its place. But it can be abused. And when that happens, it can drag you and your family into misery. Some families are so greatly in debt that their substance is eaten up by interest charges. They can never amass enough money to buy any but the smallest items for cash. They must even put dollar purchases at five and ten cent stores on the "installment plan."

The purpose of this chapter is to show you how to make credit work for you so that you won't have to work for it. If you put into practical use the information contained here, you will use credit only for specific purposes and only that type of credit plan best suited to your particular needs. You will shop for it carefully, knowing that you can save enough this way to make the time worthwhile. You will use credit in the right way—as a help to better living.

When It's O.K. to Use Credit

Almost everybody agrees that you will generally be better off if you pay cash whenever you buy something. It almost always costs you more when you buy on credit, even if the extra cost does not show up clearly on the price tag. The merchant who sells on credit in effect lends you money for a certain period, and has a right to expect interest on it. A few of those he extends credit to will not pay their bills. To cover this loss, he will charge every credit customer a certain amount extra. Moreover, he has extra bookkeeping and billing expenses he must pass on.

Some stores do not ask charge account customers to pay more than those who buy for cash. Then, however, customers who pay at once are the ones who are charged for the credit operation, and they could probably buy for less if they patronized a merchant who sold only for cash. Macy's of New York, the world's largest department store, for years has advertised that it tries, with some exceptions, to save its customers at least six percent for cash.

Accept the fact that credit is a service you must pay for, and in some cases, pay for heavily. You will then be better able to decide when this extra cost will be justified. I asked dozens of credit authorities to list when it is O.K. to buy on credit. Their consensus is:

• *When you buy something that will provide a distinct advantage and will last for years.* If you now live in a city apartment and seek a home in the suburbs where your children would have a good place to grow in, you would be foolish to wait until you saved all you would need to buy a house for

The Two Edges of Credit 37

cash; your children might be grown by the time you could do so without a mortgage.

Many labor-saving appliances fall into this category. For example, the typical housewife would probably be justified in going into debt to buy an automatic washer: The value of her time it would save would probably more than offset its cost.

• *When it is a necessity, not a luxury.* If a member of your family needs urgent medical care now, it does not make sense to wait "until you can afford it." If you live in the suburbs, far from public transportation, shops and churches, an automobile you can rely upon is probably a requirement. On the other hand, few credit authorities would advise you to borrow for a routine vacation which might be over in two weeks, but which you might be paying for during the next two years.

• *When the convenience of credit is worth more than it costs.* For example, you may wish to order from a grocery store which will deliver, and bill you later. A store may have a sale on a certain item which you need and which will be difficult to obtain later. By buying now—on credit—you may actually save a great deal of time.

• *When it costs no more to charge it.* Most people run a regular bill with their milkman. His price would be the same even if they climbed out of the bed at dawn each day to pay him on delivery. Doctors and dentists generally say they charge the same whether you pay now or later. (Some people are convinced, however, that they pay less when they discuss money matters with the doctor face to face and pay cash on the spot.)

• *When your charge account helps your tax records.* One salesman drives miles out of his way, if necessary, to fill his gasoline tank at a service station where he has a regular account. Each month he receives an itemized bill. He thus will be prepared to prove his business expenditures if he is required to do so by the income tax collector. He argues that the extra cost is more than offset by the record-keeping service he receives.

• *When it is the only way you can save regularly.* Mr. and Mrs. George White inherited a few thousand dollars which they placed in a savings account. Whenever they made an important purchase—a new television set, dishwasher, etc.—they dipped into savings. They could never restore the price of the purchase to their balance. When it dropped below a thousand dollars, they realized that they had to adopt a new policy. They decided to leave their savings intact the next time they made a major purchase and to pay for it in monthly installments. They paid more this way, but it enabled them to save the amount they would otherwise have taken from their account.

Don't Buy on Time if—

A quick test to tell whether you should make any installment purchases is suggested by the Consumer Department of the AFL-CIO. It says that the average family with small children probably can pay for one major appliance and a car at the same time. It says:

"You should not take on new installment commitments unless—

"1. You have a steady job with good prospects of wage increases.

"2. You have considered how the total price tag on the goods fits into your budget, not just the monthly payments.

"3. You don't expect any other major expense in the near future. If your wife is expecting a baby in the next few months, it's not the time to buy a new TV set!

"You may be able to take on additional installment commitments if—

"1. There is more than one wage-earner in the family.

"2. You don't hold a mortgage or other personal debts.

"3. You have some personal savings."

Are You a Good Credit Risk?

You may not realize it, but a company in your locality knows more about you than you probably imagine. Quite likely, it has a complete biography—where you were born, jobs you have held and salaries you have earned, where you live, how much rent you pay (if you are a tenant) or how much your house is worth (if you own one). It probably has a record of your charge accounts. And most important, it probably knows how you have used your credit in the past—whether you pay your debts promptly and in full.

This company may have a name like "Central Credit Bureau" or "Central Credit Exchange." Few merchants in these credit-conscious days could operate effectively without it. Here's why. Let's say a car dealer advertises a convertible for $1500 and states that you can drive it away by paying $150 down. You like the car and decide to buy it on a time-payment plan.

To make certain that you will not leave town owing him the $1350 balance, the dealer must know what kind of person you are, whether your income will enable you to make the monthly payments, and whether you have a good reputation with others you have dealt with. To conduct this investigation himself, he would have to check with your landlord, bank, present and former employers, stores where you have charge accounts, your business associates and personal friends. Such an investigation would cost much money and require many days. Meanwhile, you might change your mind and leave him without a sale.

Thanks to the local credit bureau, he need only go to the phone for a confidential report about you. He can decide in a few minutes whether you are worth the risk. Even if you are a newcomer in town—your company has just transferred you from Portland, Maine, to Dallas, Texas, for instance—a check can be made within a few hours. Most local credit bureaus are members of a nationwide network and information gathered by one exchange is made available to other bureaus that request it. Thus the Dallas car dealer can quickly learn as much about you as could a dealer in your old home town.

The existence of such an intricate set-up of efficient bureaus means one thing to you as a consumer: If you ever hope to obtain credit anywhere, keep your credit rating high.

How do you establish a credit rating, and how can you make certain that you will be able to "charge it" if the need arises? Here are the answers from Rudolph M. Severa, executive manager of the Credit Bureau of Greater New York:

"Let's say you want to open an account at your local department store. You've never bought on credit before, so your life is a clean slate as far as the credit bureaus are concerned.

"The store will ask you to fill out an application form. You'll be asked to write in your name, address and phone number, the name and address of your employer, the kind of work you do, your salary, and how long you've been employed there. You'll be asked to list the same information for previous employers.

"The store will want to know how long you've lived at your present address and where you lived before you moved to it. You'll be asked to list the name and address of your bank, and to give business and social references.

"The store may wish to check on this information itself. It may phone your employer to verify the information you gave. Some employers won't reveal how much their employees make, but a trained investigator can get a fair idea of your salary by the kind of work you do, and the type of company you are employed by. Few stenographers earn $200 a week.

"Or the store may ask the Credit Bureau to check your employment instead of doing it directly. Even if this is your very first application for credit, the store will want to clear your name through the central files of the credit bureau, to be sure you aren't hiding a prior unfavorable record, and as a protection against future unsatisfactory performance on your part in meeting obligations with other members of the credit bureau.

"Whenever you want to open a charge account or borrow from a bank in the future, you'll be asked to fill out a similar form. But now you'll be asked to list where you've had previous charge accounts, and how well you handled the first account will now be considered. Each time you sign a credit contract or make a loan, you'll add another item to your record. If you change jobs or move to a new home, get married or add dependents—all will be noted in due course.

"In addition, every member of a credit bureau is duty bound to report bad accounts. If it is forced to close out your account because you haven't paid your bills, that fact will probably also go into your record. Credit bureaus also check newspaper reports of arrests, drunken driving, etc.—factors which might indicate lack of responsibility on your part. And they regularly go over court records of judgments, bankruptcy proceedings and the like.

"In time, they will have your complete history, so it will never pay to misrepresent any facts about yourself."

How You Can Buy on Credit

If the need to borrow money arises, it's likely to be in some kind of emergency, when you cannot take time to shop thoroughly for the best deal. But it might save you a week's salary if you now consider all the ways you could borrow. Then, if the need arises later, you will know exactly where to get the money at the lowest cost to you.

If you intend to use the money to buy something (a car, furniture, electrical appliances, etc.) you generally can make credit arrangements where you make the purchase, or you may be able to borrow elsewhere and pay the merchant with cash.

If you get credit from the store itself, one of these plans will generally be used:

A REGULAR CHARGE ACCOUNT. On its face, this is a convenience for the shopper and does not cost anything extra. You buy what you want, are billed at the end of the month, and are expected to pay within 30 days. Professor Arch W. Troelstrup, head of the department of consumer education of Stephens Council, states in his textbook, "Consumer Problems and Personal Finance" (1957: McGraw-Hill Book Company, Inc., N. Y.) that its greatest advantage is convenience: You can shop quickly, need not wait for change, or fill out papers, and you need not carry large sums of cash on your person.

"A charge account is advantageous for busy people who like to order by telephone," he states. "It is a boon to those who prefer to balance their accounts at the end of each month and want a record of family purchases. This kind of credit is satisfactory if you are sure you can pay every month and if you can control the family spending. Do not use it if you have trouble making ends meet, if you are going to make heavy purchases, if you are in debt, or if you are an easy spender."

EXTENDED PAYMENT PLAN. A store may give you a longer period to pay than it allows on a straight charge account. Instead of being asked to pay in 30 days, you may be allowed to pay a fraction of the purchase price each month for three or even six months. This plan is generally promoted by merchants who sell high-priced items (clothing, furniture, appliances, etc.). It may also be known as "monthly budget plan" or "installment charge account plan."

Professor Troelstrup advises:

"Use such a plan if you want to avoid a large bill at the end of the month because these plans allow 3 to 6 months to pay, usually at no extra cost. Another advantage of a budget account is that bills are easier to pay if you save enough each month prior to payment. You can also take advantage of sales, even though you do not have cash in hand at the time of a sale.

The Two Edges of Credit

"There are some disadvantages. You may pay a 'service charge' if you take more than 90 days to pay, and you may have to make a down payment. Some service charges are deceptive. A service charge may be $3 per $100 of purchased goods. If this is repaid in six monthly installments, the discount rate is 12 percent because you have the use of only half the money during the life of the loan. Another disadvantage is that it is easy to overbuy."

REVOLVING CREDIT. This type of charge account plan is fairly new. A store may decide to grant you a credit of $500, meaning that you may charge any amount up to that sum. Each month, you pay on the account—perhaps a sixth of what you owe. Professor Troelstrup says that "This form of credit also may lead to wasteful buying. If you used it continuously, you would be in debt permanently."

INSTALLMENT PAYMENT PLAN. This often goes by the name of "Easy Payment Plan" or "Monthly Budget Plan." You make a down payment—perhaps 10 percent of the purchase price—and sign a contract agreeing to pay the remainder in monthly installments over a period which may last as long as three years.

Professor Troelstrup makes this analysis:

"Installment buying enables you to have things for which you might otherwise have to wait years. Payments are made easier by stretching them over a long period of time. It might be called 'forced budgeting'—an aid to nonbudgeters.

"The big disadvantage of installment buying is that it may tie up a portion of your income for a considerable period. The future payments may be needed for other unforeseen needs and emergencies. You may also be tempted to buy expensive things that you do not really need.

"Installment rates are higher than they appear. Suppose you buy a $300 stove and pay $60 down. A salesman might figure the bill as follows:

"Down payment: $60

"Length of time: 12 months

"Monthly payment: $22

"Total it, and you will discover that you will pay $324 ($60 down plus 12 payments of $22) for the $300 stove. The extra $24 is the carrying charge. This accounts to a true interest rate of about 18 percent a year on the balance due. This is the price you pay for getting the stove one year earlier than otherwise."

The Credit Union National Association points out that if you buy merchandise on time, you ordinarily sign either a chattel mortgage, a conditional sales contract, a bailment lease or a security agreement. It says:

"When you sign, you agree:

"To pay your debt in installments, including all charges stated in the contract. The creditor sets the charges.

"That while you get possession of the merchandise, the creditor owns it until you pay him in full.

"Not to sell the mcerchandise, or move it away, or include it in another transaction.

"To be responsible for loss or damage. This is why insurance is often required.

"That if you fail to make payments as promised, the creditor can take back the merchandise or hold you liable for the entire unpaid balance. He can do this even if you owe only ONE payment.

"You should always do four things before you sign:

1. "Compare prices. Get cost for cash and time price (including cost and all charges) from several dealers. A high cash price may include extra charges. A low cash price may mean high financing charges.

2. "Size up your dealer. If he insists on financing instead of a cash deal, watch out! It usually means he makes an extra profit on the finance charges.

3. "Read the contract, and ask questions. Be sure all the spaces are filled in, and that you understand the terms.

4. "Find out who the creditor will be. The contract may be

turned over to a bank or a sales finance company. When the finance company takes the contract, it does not take responsibility for the seller's good faith. To bring action against the dealer, you will probably have to go to court."

How You Can Borrow Money

Instead of using the store's credit facilities you can also borrow the money needed to make the purchase at various lending institutions. You would also apply to these lenders if you sought money to pay hospital or medical expenses, to clear up bills, pay taxes, pay for your youngsters' school tuition, or for other purposes.

Here are the most common types of loan you can get.

SAVINGS LOANS. You may obtain these at the savings and loan association or bank where you maintain a savings account. You can make a loan simply by showing your passbook. Of course, you cannot borrow more than you have in your account. You continue to draw interest on the amount you have deposited, so that the actual rate of interest you pay for the convenience of the loan may amount to only 1, 2 or 3 percent.

Why borrow money when you can take the cash out of your savings account? If you could be sure that you would pay back the same amounts into your account each month as you are forced to pay when you borrow, there would be little reason to do so. But most persons need a spur to make them save.

INSURANCE LOANS. Most policies, except the straight term type, have cash surrender values—amounts you could receive if you discontinued the policy. Using your policy as security, your insurance company will lend you a sum no greater than this cash value. The company will not lose any money if you default on the loan, hence can keep interest rates down. You may pay about 6 percent per year. Meanwhile, however, cash invested in your policy continues to draw dividends of perhaps 3 percent.

COLLATERAL LOANS. Most commercial banks also will lend at relatively low rates if you submit insurance policies, bank books, stocks, bonds or other assets which they could turn into cash if you failed to pay what you owe.

Suppose you are holding 100 shares of stock to help you pay for your son's college education. A bank might lend you 50 percent of the market value and charge you 6 percent interest. However, if the price of the shares dropped so much that they might no longer be sufficient security, the bank might ask you to pay some of the loan at once. Thus you might have to sell your stock at an unfavorable price to cover the loan.

Collateral loans are commonly made for three or six-month periods. You usually can renew them at the end of this time.

CONVENTIONAL BANK LOANS. These are also known as personal loans, home improvement loans, car purchase loans, etc. If your credit rating is good, and your income is large enough, you may be able to borrow as much as $3,500 for periods up to five years. Loans of this type may be made on your own signature, or you may need co-makers who promise to make good if you default.

True interest rates may be 10 percent and higher. If you are allowed a long repayment period, your monthly payments will be less and your total interest payments will be greater. Along with the loan, some banks include a life insurance policy for the amount owed so that the debt will be paid in full if you die.

CONSUMER FINANCE COMPANY LOANS. These companies often deal with borrowers who are poor risks or cannot get conventional bank loans. The companies often borrow from the banks themselves to get the money they lend you. On top of the interest they must pay, they must add the costs of their own overhead, salaries, advertising and profit.

These companies generally charge a flat percentage rate of

interest per month. In New York State, for example, private loan companies charge 2½ percent per month on the first $100 you owe, 2 percent on the next $200, and ½ of 1 percent on any remainder of the unpaid balance.

CREDIT UNIONS. These are cooperative thrift and loan associations in which savings of members are used to provide other members with low-cost loans in time of need. Explains Jerry Voorhis, executive director of the Cooperative League of the U.S.A.: "Employees of a firm, members of an association or residents of a well-defined community may organize a credit union. In rural areas people often organize credit unions on a community-wide basis. In the city the field of membership may be a labor union or a church parish. In some states the law permits a cooperative to be a member of the credit union composed of its members.

"Maximum interest rate is 1 percent per month on the unpaid balance. This usually includes life insurance for the amount of the loan. Congress has set $750 as the maximum credit union loan which could be granted with the borrower's signature as the only security. State credit union acts vary. The Illinois law, for example, sets $500 as the maximum."

PERSONAL "LOAN SHARKS." Many of these exist where small loan laws do not exist or are inadequate. In many business offices and factories, and in some lower-class neighborhoods, individuals have set up their own private businesses, lending money to fellow employees or neighbors in desperate need.

A common interest rate is 20 percent *per week:* If you borrow $5 today, you will be required to pay back $6 a week from now. If you fail to pay, the amount you owe will be added to your balance, and the interest will be computed on the total.

One man lost his job and borrowed $100 from a "loan shark" to tide him over until he could obtain another one. He had to wait nine weeks. By then, thanks to the "loan shark's" method of compounding interest, the man owed $515.98. The interest due each week was more than the original loan.

How to Figure What Credit Will Cost You

You are not in a good position to judge whether to pay cash or buy on credit unless you know exactly what the credit will cost you. Surprisingly, many people who borrow from banks or loan companies and consistently buy on the installment plan lack even a vague idea of what the privilege costs them. For example, salesmen for furniture stores often meet young couples who do not care to know the full price of an item; they merely wish to know "how much per month" they must pay.

The Boston Better Business Bureau has devised a simple way to determine the annual rate you pay when you buy on the installment plan. This can be obtained by dividing the total cost of the credit for a year by the total amount of credit extended for a year.

Say you buy a television set on sale for $118. To get it, you need only pay $10 down, and $10 a month for twelve months. Since you will wind up paying $130, the credit will cost $12. Therefore you might say offhand that $12 represents one-tenth of the advertised price and that the interest rate is 10 percent per year. But you would be mistaken. The annual rate of interest is almost twice that percentage.

To arrive at the exact rate, first determine the total cost of the credit—in this case, $12. It is the difference between what you borrow and what you must repay.

Next determine how much credit you are extended *for the entire period*. In this case, it would be $120 only for the first month. It would drop to $110 the second month, $100 the third and so on. Add the amounts owed at the end of each month and divide by 12. Result: The average amount of credit actually extended for the entire year—in this case, $65.

Now divide the cost of credit ($12) by the actual credit

($65). The annual interest rate you must pay for the privilege of buying on time is found to be 18½ percent.

Credit unions and consumer finance companies state their interest charges as a monthly percentage rate on the actual unpaid balance. Say you borrow $200 from a finance company January 1, and the monthly interest rate is 2 percent. At the end of the month, you will owe $4 in interest. At that time, you pay the $4 plus $40 of the principal. At the end of the next month, you will owe interest of $3.20—2 percent of the unpaid balance which is $160.

It is easy to determine the yearly interest rate when this method is used. You simply multiply the monthly rate by twelve. One percent a month amounts to 12 percent a year and 2 percent a month is 24 percent a year. But it is important to realize that this interest rate is applied to successively lower amounts of principal as you make your monthly payments.

When you have exact information on the cost of credit, you can directly compare what it will cost you to buy on time or to borrow the money from a consumer finance company or other lending institution. If you always compare actual percentage rates, you may save considerable money.

How to Compare Car Financing Costs

Shown on the next page is how to compare information you get from several financing organizations. The sample figures show how to use the chart. They do not necessarily represent current prices or payments.

How You Can Keep Out of Trouble with Your Creditors

Obviously, a merchant or money-lender wants to know whether you have the ability to pay the bill you are contracting. This depends upon two things—your income and how many other bills you must pay out of it each month. As a gen-

Facts You Need	Example	Dealer's Arrangement	Bank	Other Source
Terms	⅓ down, 30 months, 6% interest a year			
Total cost of car, including all extras and taxes	$3000.00	$	$	$
Deduct down payment:				
Trade-in allowance $880.00				
Cash 328.00				
Total	1208.00			
Balance due after down payment	$1792.00	$	$	$
Insurance costs throughout contract period	206.00			
Total fees for credit investigation and other services	2.00			
Total amount (principal) to be financed	$2000.00	$	$	$
Financing charge over period of payments (Sample figure, 2½ years @ 6%)	300.00			
Total amount owed on contract	$2300.00	$	$	$
Number of monthly payments	30			
Amount per payment	$76.67			

Source: Money Management Institute, Household Finance Corp.

eral rule, banks and other lenders dislike to extend credit that will bring your monthly payments on all your outstanding loans, installment plan commitments, etc., to more than 20 percent of your total take home pay. Your regular monthly mortgage expenses are not included in this computation.

Example: You earn $600 per month, and already have committed yourself to pay $80 per month for an automobile and $30 per month for a refrigerator. A banker might be willing to make a small loan that you could pay off at the rate of $10 per month, but he probably would not let you get deeper into debt. Here is another way of looking at it: Suppose your monthly loan payments for next year will amount to 20 percent of your income. You would have to work for more than ten weeks—and spend not a cent of your salary on anything else—to clear up your obligations. Obviously you are in debt deeply enough.

The second important point the merchant wants to know is whether you pay your bills on time or whether he will have to threaten you with lawsuits to get his money. Says Mr. Severa:

"Credit bureaus keep a careful check on your payment records. Say you have a charge account with your local department store and consistently pay your bills within 30 days. You are listed in the top category. If you pay within from 30 to 60 days, you are about average. If you take from 60 to 90 days, you are regarded as fair pay, and if you take more than 120 days, you are definitely a poor payer. If you consistently take longer than four months to pay your bills, don't be shocked if you receive a flat 'no' the next time you want to use your credit."

What if you get into a credit jam and find yourself overwhelmed with bills you can't pay? Answers Mr. Severa: "There is only one thing to do: Frankly tell your creditors that you have over-extended yourself—and let them know that you intend to do the best you can.

"Never ignore your creditors' requests for payment. Try to pay something. Even if you pay only part of what you owe, at least you are demonstrating that you intend to pay the rest eventually. If you have misused your charge account at a store, pay at least a few dollars each week and let the credit manager know that you are determined not to charge anything else until your current debts are paid. If you owe on a bank loan, at least pay the interest. Never let conditions reach the point where your creditors go to your employer with a court order directing that he turn your wages over to them in order to pay your debts. Some employers fire the worker whose wages are garnisheed. They regard this inability to pay debts as proof that the employee is irresponsible.

"A basic point to remember: Few banks, merchants or money-lenders want to persecute the person who has got himself into financial hot water. Writing threatening letters, employing lawyers, obtaining court fees all take time and cost money. They would rather deal with you pleasantly and stretch a point, if necessary, to help you get out of a jam. But you have to show them that you fully intend to pay."

What About Credit Cards?

These little cards have become a national institution in less than the past dozen years. You could arrive penniless in a strange city, stay at the best hotels, eat at the best restaurants and buy armloads of goods at the most fashionable stores all on the strength of this magic paper in your hands.

Seemingly, almost anyone with a good credit rating can now get a card. The major credit card companies (such as Diner's Club and American Express Co.) advertise vigorously for customers, make application blanks widely available and set up booths at railroad stations and other places where masses of people can be found. If your application is approved, you become a member for a modest annual fee ($5 or $6). You receive a membership card and a list of restaurants, hotels, stores and an almost unbelievable variety of merchants—florists, booksellers, druggists, car rental agencies, etc.—who will honor it. You buy what you want, show your card and sign a sales slip, and walk out without paying a cent. The bill is forwarded to the credit-card firm, which takes from 2 to 10 percent as its commission, and then includes it with all your other credit card purchases in a single bill each month.

Impartial credit authorities say that the success of these plans proves that they have filled a need. This can be said in their favor:

- *They provide a painless way of keeping records.* If you travel or entertain for business purposes, you might find it inconvenient to ask for receipts whenever you made a cash purchase. Yet you must show receipts as proof of the business expenditures you deduct on your income tax return. The credit card companies provide you with the detailed record you need.
- *They are a safe substitute for money.* A traveller need not carry large sums which might be lost or stolen.
- *They provide excellent identification.* Your possession of a credit card proves that you have been investigated and have been found to be a good credit risk. Many hotels, etc., will cash personal checks when you produce your card.

For individuals striving to set up a sound personal financial program, however, the regular use of a credit card may entail some hazards. For example:

- *They provide a constant temptation to over-spend.* Generally, only the most expensive establishments honor credit cards, because their prices are high enough to cover the commission they must pay the credit card companies. At a "credit card restaurant," you will be tempted to order extra drinks and a more expensive meal—and to leave a larger tip—because you don't have to pay with cash from your pocket.
- *Your expenses can easily get out of hand.* Some people find it difficult to remember the amount of the credit company bill they will have to pay each month. They forget what they have charged, and discover with a shock that their total bill amounts to more than they had expected. To pay it, they may have to make other sacrifices. Holders of credit cards may find it more difficult to observe a primary rule for a sound personal financial program—"If you can't afford it, do without."

"Ten Commandments for Borrowers"

Here are "Ten Commandments" recommended by the Credit Union National Association for all who seek to borrow money or buy on time:

1. No matter what interest rates are quoted, find out what the credit or loan will actually cost in money. This is the first thing to do.

2. Before you sign any papers, make sure all the figures are entered correctly. Don't leave any blank spaces to be filled in later.

3. Question all insurance charges. Find out what kind of insurance you are buying, and exactly what it covers. Many different insurance rackets have been reported.

4. On installment purchases, you may owe the payments to some other firm, not the dealer. Find out who it is, and if it is a reputable firm. If you have any doubts, check with the Better Business Bureau.

5. Read the note or contract to see what penalties are imposed for late payments. This is where many dishonest lenders make money.

6. See if there are any other extra charges specified in the note or contract. Don't skip the fine print, or you may be sorry.

7. Read what is said about repossession in a time-payment contract. Do you get a fair notice before the item is repossessed? What repossession charges can be levied against you? This is important.

8. Understand clearly what security you are giving. On a purchase, find out if it includes other merchandise you have bought previously. Above all, look to see if the note or contract gives your creditor the right to collect your salary through a wage assignment.

9. Make sure you do not sign away any of your legal rights or guarantees, such as the right to refuse merchandise which is not as promised.

10. See if there is provision for a refund of interest or carrying charges if you complete the payments ahead of schedule.

chapter four

HOW TO
PUT YOUR EXTRA CASH TO WORK

A planned savings program can earn more money for your family. This chapter tells where and how to save effectively

A young married couple can look forward to more security today than ever before in history. If you lose your job, you can get unemployment compensation. If you become disabled or seriously ill, your hospital or medical insurance will pay some—perhaps all—of your bills. If you cause an automobile accident and injure someone severely, insurance may cover all damage claims and the accident may not cost you a penny. When you become 60 or 65, a retirement plan sponsored by your employer or union may guarantee at least a small check each month. In any event, the Social Security program will probably assure you of a monthly payment.

Hardly any development of an unexpected nature could reduce you to absolute, abject poverty. Thanks to security programs sponsored by the government, employers, unions and others, you probably will always know where your next meals at least are coming from.

"All these things are a great help, but they are not a complete answer," says Norman Strunk, executive vice president of the United States Savings and Loan League. "They are protective devices which give partial, minimum security. They will prevent catastrophes—but they cannot give you the good things you want in life.

"They will not enable you to make a down payment on a home—to give your family a place of its own, to provide the atmosphere you want your children to grow up in. They won't send your youngsters to college. They won't give you the dishwasher, clothes-washer or clothes-dryer that can take drudgery out of housework. They won't buy a new car or new living room furniture, enable you to vacation at the seashore, travel to Europe, or even to live in reasonable comfort when you retire.

"Only your savings will do that—the money you yourself set aside out of your earnings. And that is why a savings account is more important than ever. For although we have more built-in security and protection against want, we also have greater desires than ever before. You do not want just to avoid living in desperate want and poverty. You seek to enjoy the good things which have become part of the American way. But no amount of planned security will give you those things. You will have to provide them for yourself, and out of your own savings."

What Planned Savings Will Do for You

If you start a systematic savings program—one in which you put aside a certain amount of your earnings each pay day—you will easily achieve a variety of objectives, says Helen White, executive secretary of the National Thrift Committee. For example:

• *A planned Savings Program will give you peace of mind.* It is a rare family which does not experience at least one major crisis every few years, when it needs extra funds to tide it over a rough spot. Perhaps it is unemployment: Even if you are secure in your job, you may be laid off due to conditions—

How to Put Your Extra Cash to Work

like materials shortages due to strikes elsewhere—over which you have no control. Or you may have unexpectedly large medical or dental expenditures for which insurance compensates you only in part.

The peace of mind savings can give you translates itself into freedom of action. Two men worked alongside each other for a firm which was bought by a large corporation. The first had extensive savings; the second had none. As rumors swept the concern that its workers would lose their jobs, the first knew that his savings could support his family while he sought new employment. The second became almost a nervous wreck worrying about what he might do if the reports were true. Fortunately, the rumors were proved to be false after circulating for months. But no one could doubt that the first man's savings accounted at least partly for his feeling of security under difficult circumstances.

• *A planned Savings Program provides buying power.* You can take advantage of opportunities as they occur. A housewife planned to buy a winter coat. In August, a local shop advertised coats for $50. It said it would sell the same coats in the Fall for $80. By withdrawing $50 from her account, she took advantage of the opportunity.

Another couple saw sales in October featuring merchandise at 30 percent less than they would have to pay in December. Because they had the cash, they did their Christmas shopping early, and saved a whopping sum.

An advertising man in Detroit was suddenly transferred to San Francisco and had to sell his outboard motorboat quickly. A fellow-employee with a savings account was able to get it for cash at half the price it might have cost otherwise.

When middle-aged people review their lives, most can see many opportunities they missed because they lacked capital. There might have been a chance to invest in a sound, new business, a chance to buy real estate at attractive prices, a chance to purchase a special stock at a bargain level. They know from experience the value of having purchasing power in reserve.

• *A planned Savings Program provides earning power.* Benjamin Franklin, in one of his wisest moments, said that "money begets money and its offspring begets more." He meant that if you leave your savings at interest, they will continue to grow ever greater and greater.

Franklin proved that himself. In 1791, he bequeathed $5,000 to the residents of Boston with the restriction that they permit it to earn interest for a century. When that time was up, the original sum had grown to $400,000—dramatic proof of the earning power of compound interest.

So great is this power that, if you could leave money untouched for 23 years at 4½% interest, compounded quarterly, it will be three times greater at the end of the period than it was at the beginning. If you place a dollar in a savings account at the age of 25, it will probably increase more than five times before you reach retirement age. Even the man who begins a belated retirement program and opens a savings account at 50 will see his initial deposit virtually double at 4½% interest by the time he is 65.

• *A planned Savings Program is necessary for our way of life.* Under our capitalist system, savings of private individuals are needed to run our factories, utilities, banks, insurance companies and other enterprises. Without mortgages which are financed by savings, most Americans would be unable to buy homes. Many small businessmen would be unable to keep their doors open. Many large corporations would be unable to expand, perhaps even extend credit to their customers, for savings are often used to tide a business over until it is paid for merchandise it has sold. In fact, without savings our whole economic structure would crumble. Thus your savings, in addition to doing a valuable job for you personally, also perform a patriotic service.

How to Put Your Extra Cash to Work

What Will Your Money Earn?

Here are the average annual dividend or interest payments from selected types of investments for every year since 1940.

Year	Savings and Loan Accounts	Savings Deposits in Mutual Savings Banks	Savings Deposits in Commercial Banks	United States Bonds
1940	3.3	2.0	1.3	2.2
1941	3.1	1.9	1.3	2.2
1942	3.0	1.9	1.1	2.5
1943	2.9	1.9	0.9	2.5
1944	2.8	1.8	0.9	2.5
1945	2.5	1.7	0.8	2.4
1946	2.4	1.7	0.8	2.2
1947	2.3	1.7	0.9	2.3
1948	2.3	1.8	0.9	2.4
1949	2.3	1.9	0.9	2.3
1950	2.5	2.0	0.9	2.3
1951	2.6	2.1	1.1	2.6
1952	2.7	2.4	1.1	2.7
1953	2.8	2.5	1.1	2.9
1954	2.9	2.6	1.3	2.5
1955	2.9	2.7	1.4	2.8
1956	3.0	2.8	1.6	3.1
1957	3.3	3.0	2.1	3.5
1958	3.5	3.1	2.2	3.4
1959	3.7	3.2	2.4	4.1

Savings and Loan Associations: Effective rate of dividends, i.e., dividends distributed relative to average savings capital, based on data of members of FHLB System, mutual savings banks "per deposit" rates reported by Association of Mutual Savings Banks; commercial banks; effective interest rate, based on data of Federal Reserve Board and Federal Deposit Insurance Corporation.

How Much Should You be Saving?

There is almost unanimous agreement among experts—investment advisers, home economists, etc.—that a couple should strive to accumulate six months' earnings in savings which they might withdraw easily if necessary, and which will not fluctuate in value. With half a year's income set aside, you will have substantial protection against almost any ordinary financial crisis. You will be able to take advantage of buying opportunities that arise. And you will have a regular, extra income: Invest six months' savings at 4% interest, and each year you will receive the equivalent of a full week's salary.

Home economists say that the six-month figure is an average one. Some families will have more savings; others will have less. Newly-married couples may have heavy expenses in furnishing a home and may be unable to save much. But some authorities recommend that you place at least 5 percent of your earnings into a savings account, regardless of your other expenses, until you have six months' income in your nest egg.

Since the purpose of this account is to provide for emergencies, at times your balance may drop below the six months' figure. If that happens, try as soon as possible to restore your balance to its previous level. Or you might convert other savings—stocks and bonds, for example—and put them where you can get at them easily if necessary.

The six-month figure is a minimum, of course. You may need more to meet special expenses—for example, to make a down payment on a home, to pay your children's college expenses, to provide a cushion for your retirement. But only after you have a substantial amount in a savings account should you consider investing elsewhere where the possibility of profit—and of loss—is greater.

What to Look for Before Opening a Savings Account

Victor H. Nyborg, president of the Association of Better Business Bureaus, Inc., says that savings accounts should fulfill four requirements:

• *Your money should be safe.* You should be certain that you will get back every dollar you place into an account. You have this assurance when you deposit your money in any of the regulated savings institutions in the country—in savings and loan associations, savings banks, commercial banks, credit unions—where Federal or State authorities have set up safeguards and Federal or State Insurance covering accounts up to $10,000 per depositor is in effect. The Federal Deposit Insurance Corporation and Federal Savings and Loan Insurance Corporation are the official U. S. government agencies which insure. Be cautious of institutions which claim to be "commercially insured" or just "insured."

Institutions operating under Federal or State laws must submit to periodic examinations. Government examiners check thoroughly to insure that deposits are invested legally and that the institution can meet all ordinary demands of depositors.

• *You should be able to withdraw your savings easily.* In order to pay interest on the money you deposit, all savings institutions must lend it to others at higher interest rates. These borrowers may be families seeking mortgages on homes, businessmen or individuals needing personal loans. In most cases these loans will not be paid back for months or years. Therefore, a part of a savings institution's deposits will be tied up for long periods.

But suppose all its depositors suddenly decided to withdraw their savings. Their money would be out on loans in order to earn interest, and probably could not be recalled in time to pay them in full. For that reason, banks and savings institutions are members of a federal government-sponsored reserve banking system and can borrow substantial amounts to meet their cash withdrawal requests. In addition, all banks and savings institutions keep the right to require savers to give advance notice of withdrawals. But it is extremely unlikely that they will exercise this right. As a matter of every-day practice, any insured savings institution keeps more than enough funds on hand to meet normal withdrawal demands, and a depositor can be reasonably sure that he will be able to withdraw all his funds immediately without waiting.

• *Your money should earn satisfactory dividends or interest.* One institution may pay twice the interest on your money as will another. Over the years, this factor can make a tremendous difference. Say you deposit $1,000 in "Institution A" which pays 2% interest and compounds it semi-annually. It will take almost 35 years for your $1,000 to double. Deposit the same amount in "Institution B," paying 4%, compounded semi-annually, and it will take less than 17½ years for the sum to double. At the end of 35 years you will have $2,000 in the first institution. But you will have more than $4,000 in the second. Thus the interest or dividend rate is vital.

Why this difference in rates? It is primarily due to how the savings institution uses your deposits. An institution which lends at high interest rates can afford to pay more. Another institution, limited in the kind of loans it can make, may be unable to invest so profitably. Thus it cannot pay such attractive interest rates. However, it is wise to check carefully if an institution offers to pay exceptionally high interest or dividend rates.

• *The savings institution should be convenient to your home or place of business.* Many experts argue that you will be encouraged to save regularly if you have an accessible place in which to deposit funds. However, most institutions now make it easy to make deposits and withdrawals by mail. This method is sometimes the most convenient of all since you can conduct your business at any hour and during any day of the week.

Where Should You Place Your Savings?

There are four major types of savings institutions. Below are the facts about each.

SAVINGS AND LOAN ASSOCIATIONS. There are 6,230 such associations throughout the country, and they are the fastest-growing savings institutions in the United States. At the end of 1945, they had only 7.4 billions in deposits, compared to 29.9 billions in commercial banks. But in 1959, they were up to 54.7 billions, were rapidly gaining on the commercial banks, which now had 62.7 billions, and they had 26,618,000 accounts in force.

A savings and loan association generally is a "specialty shop" with but two functions: It offers you a place where you can invest your savings and it makes real estate loans—most of them first mortgage loans on single family homes to people in your community.

A savings and loan association may operate under different names. In your section, one may be known as a building and loan association, a savings and loan company, a cooperative bank, savings association, or homestead association.

Most associations are owned by the people who save or invest with them. When you open an account, you become a part-owner in effect, and are entitled to a share of the earnings after all operating expenses are paid. Your share is paid to you in the form of dividends. In some cases, the associations are owned by investors who advanced the capital to start them.

Savings and loan associations generally pay higher dividends (or interest rates) than other institutions. In 1960, most paid between $3\frac{1}{2}$ and $4\frac{1}{2}\%$, while the rate paid by commercial banks varied from $2\frac{1}{2}$ to 3%. These higher rates are possible because associations generally have lower expenses and are permitted by law to invest more of their assets in more profitable investments. They make most of their loans to families in the community to enable them to buy or build single-family homes. The loans are secured by a first mortgage and are paid off at so much per month over 10 to 30-year periods.

The fact that home-owners continually make payments to an association to reduce their mortgages gives it a constant source of money to satisfy depositors withdrawing their funds. Each association also keeps from 10 to 15 percent of its assets in cash, and in government bonds which can quickly be turned into cash, in order to meet depositors' demands. In addition, an association can borrow up to 50% of the total in its savings accounts from the Federal Home Loan Bank.

These safeguards mean that you will ordinarily be able to withdraw your funds without waiting whenever you choose. However, like other savings institutions, an association has a legal right to defer payments.

The Federal Savings and Loan Insurance Corporation, which insures savings accounts in savings and loan associations, is an agency of the federal government. Created by Congress in 1934, it is managed by three trustees who are appointed by the President and confirmed by the Senate. It is the same type of agency as the Federal Deposit Insurance Corporation, which insures the deposits in commercial banks and most savings banks up to $10,000.

If an insured institution defaults, the FSLIC will pay each insured holder as soon as possible. The language in the FSLIC payoff procedures for account holders is identical to the FDIC procedures for commercial bank depositors. Both corporations provide that payment will be either in cash or by crediting the saver with an account in an operating, insured institution. In the 26 years since the FSLIC was set up, no person with a savings account covered by it has lost a penny. In the few cases when an insured institution has been in trouble, the FSLIC has always moved in promptly to protect savers and to make funds immediately available. The excellent record in this connection is assurance to the public that savings and loan associations will continue to make the savers' funds available when wanted or needed.

In a few states, the state government provides for insurance of accounts under state supervision.

MUTUAL SAVINGS BANKS. These instiutions are concentrated in the northeastern section of the United States. They generally perform more financial services than most savings associations. Many have safe deposit boxes, sell money orders, cashiers' checks and travelers' checks, and operate school and payroll savings plans and Christmas and Vacation Clubs. Savings banks in Massachusetts, New York and Connecticut also sell life insurance. These institutions had approximately $35,000,000 in savings at the end of 1959. Like most savings and loan associations, they are owned by their depositors.

Deposits in mutual savings banks generally are also insured by a federal or state agency—by the Federal Deposit Insurance Corporation or by State Insurance firms such as the Mutual Savings Central Fund of Massachusetts which was set up under State law. Terms of such insurance state that if a bank cannot meet your demands, the insurance corporation will pay the amount of your insured deposit in cash or will open an account in another insured bank with an amount equal to your insured deposit in the old bank. These provisions are basically the same as those for other savings institutions.

The state laws generally specify exactly how savings banks may invest their assets. They must maintain a certain percentage in cash and government securities, and may invest certain other percentages in mortgages and a selected list of bonds, preferred and common stocks. On the average, savings banks pay lower interest rates than do savings and loan associations, but higher rates than those paid by commercial banks. Depositors may be required to give thirty to ninety days' notice before withdrawing their funds. In times of emergency, the

State may also specify an additional waiting period for withdrawals. But these clauses are rarely invoked, and depositors as a rule can get all their savings upon demand.

COMMERCIAL BANKS. These are privately-owned corporations which strive to pay profits to stockholders who have invested their capital. In addition to servicing savings accounts, a typical bank offers checking accounts and safe deposit boxes. It manages investments of individuals while they are alive and their estates when they die. It makes loans to businessmen, industries, individuals buying on credit, etc. It provides other services for businessmen. For example, it may serve as a check-cashing institution and pay out cash to employees who receive payroll checks from their employers.

Commercial banks may be established under Federal or State law. The former are known as "national banks"; the latter, "state banks." In either case, savings deposits may be insured by the Federal Deposit Insurance Corporation. Provisions of this insurance are similar to those covering accounts in savings and loan associations and savings banks: Whenever an insured bank is closed for liquidation because it cannot meet its depositors' demands, the insurance corporation will pay the insured deposits as soon as possible either by cash or by transferring the savings account to another insured bank. Since 1934, the Federal Deposit Insurance Corporation has stepped in to protect savings depositors of 436 commercial banks throughout the country, but no saver has ever lost a penny and in only a few instances experienced a delay or inconvenience in getting his money.

Commercial banks are required by law to maintain a high percentage of assets in the form of cash, easily-sold U. S. government securities, and loans which will be paid either on demand or within periods of three to six months. The primary purpose of this liquidity is to enable them to pay out cash instantly if their checking account depositors—who receive no interest—should suddenly make wholesale withdrawals.

In emergencies, commercial banks might require savers to wait for a month or longer before they could get the full amount of their savings. As in the case of other savings institutions, however, this provision would probably not be used widely except in a depression even more serious than the one in the 1930s. As a practical matter, you can withdraw your savings whenever you wish.

When you open a savings account in a commercial bank, you enter a contract which makes you the lender and the bank the borrower. It agrees to pay you a stipulated interest rate. However, because a high proportion of its assets must be kept where they draw low rates of interest or none at all, and because it strives to earn profits for its owners, a commercial bank generally pays lower interest rates than do competitive institutions.

CREDIT UNIONS. These are non-profit organizations of people who save their money together and make low-cost loans to each other, for good purposes. Only persons with a common bond (such as employment in the same factory, membership in the same church), can form a credit union, or belong to it. To become a member, however, you need only fill out an application card, pay a fee—usually 25 cents—and buy one savings share (usually $5). Or you must agree to make regular deposits toward the first share. The credit union's board of directors must formally approve your application, and a passbook is then issued to you.

Like other savings institutions, credit unions operate under federal or state laws. Some states permit them to accept simple deposits but savings usually consist of share deposits. Dividends are paid on these when earned after required reserves are set aside. These dividends are paid on "share months"— for every month each full share is held during the period. Only those amounts on deposit at the end of the period are counted. The average annual dividend rate in most credit unions is about 4 percent. Many credit unions also refund part of the interest paid to borrowers.

"Investing in America" with Savings Bonds

For ordinary savers, the U. S. Government sells "E" and "H" Bonds. These always have a fixed dollar value and do not fluctuate in price, as do the bonds of industrial corporations or even U. S. Government Bonds which are sold primarily to institutions. At any given time, you can cash them in and obtain exactly what they are worth.

Series "E" bonds are available in denominations of $25, $50, $100, $200, $500, $1,000 and $10,000. But when you buy them, you pay 25 percent less—$18.75 for the $25 bond, $37.50 for the $50 bond, etc. They mature seven years and nine months from the first day of the month of purchase. Although they yield $3.75 percent interest if held to maturity, they yield less if you cash them in before that time.

No one person can buy bonds totalling more than $10,000 face value in any one calendar year in his name alone. But individuals can also be co-owners with others and each co-ownership is limited to $10,000 per calendar year.

E bonds can be redeemed any time after sixty days from their date of issue. But if you redeem them during the first six months of ownership, they draw no interest. You will get back only the amount you paid.

H bonds come in units of $500, $1,000, $5,000 and $10,000. Investors receive their interest on a regular basis, instead of waiting until the end of a maturity period, as is required with E bonds. H bonds, therefore, always sell at their face amount.

The same provisions apply for buying H bonds as for E bonds. You cannot buy more than $10,000 worth in a calendar year, but you can be co-owner with others. You must hold H bonds for six months, and must give a calendar month's written notice before redeeming them.

H bonds mature ten years after purchase. Interest payments are made semi-annually. You must hold them at least two years before you begin to draw interest at the rate of $4 annually for each $100 you have invested.

A possible advantage of buying E bonds is that you need not pay taxes on the interest that accrues until you redeem them. In addition, under Treasury Department regulations you can hold them after their normal maturity and continue to earn interest upon their maturity value. Thus a couple might buy E bonds and defer paying taxes on the interest until they retire. The tax rate then might be considerably lower than if they redeemed the bonds in their years of high earnings.

Holders of E bonds may also switch to H bonds before the end of the maturity period without paying taxes on the interest the E bonds had earned until the H bonds mature or are redeemed, whichever is sooner. So they get another ten years, during which time they can use the full amount of the interest earned on the E bonds to earn more interest.

Savings Bonds are often recommended to individuals who will probably keep them to maturity and beyond. Since they do not give as good a return when held for short periods, many investment experts do not advise them for couples who might need their savings for emergencies.

Five Ways to Be a Successful Saver

Norman Strunk of the United States Savings and Loan League advises:

• *Open an account as soon as possible.* Many people seem unable to take this first important step, but without it their good intentions are futile. You need not begin with a large sum. Often only $1 will open an account. Savings institutions will start your account with this amount because they know that savers find it easier to make other deposits once an account exists.

Opening an account probably will take only a few minutes. You need only give an officer of the institution your name and address and the name and place of your business. You will be given a passbook which will serve as a record of your deposits and withdrawals. You will be advised to guard it carefully, for you will need it to make withdrawals. You will be asked to report immediately to the savings institution if it is lost or misplaced, so that others may not use it to take funds from your account.

• *Establish regular saving habits.* This is the key to successful saving. Try to make your savings automatic. Then regular amounts will go into your account regularly, and you won't have to make a decision about it every time. You can establish automatic savings patterns in various ways:

See if your employer has a payroll deduction plan. If so, he will apply a certain amount of your paycheck to a savings institution or towards the purchase of a U. S. Savings Bond. If your employer has no payroll deduction plan in effect in your place of business, perhaps an official at your savings institution can arrange to apply regular paycheck deductions to your savings account. Generally, employers heartily approve of payroll deduction plans because they know that steady savers are steady employees.

In making your monthly mortgage payments, add a regular amount to the payment and apply it to your savings account. Savings and loan associations and savings banks, which hold most of the nation's home mortgages, will usually take mortgage payments and savings deposits at the same time.

Bill yourself every month. One couple has a regular date for paying monthly telephone, utility and medical bills, mortgage payments, etc. While writing checks for these items, the husband habitually also draws a check for their savings account.

• *Take advantage of deposit and withdrawal dates.* Many institutions will credit you from the first of the month if you make a deposit before the tenth, or even later. Take advantage of these days of grace if you can.

Remember, too, that your money must be on deposit for a full period to receive interest—for example, from January 10 to June 30 in order to draw a semi-annual interest payment. If you make a withdrawal May 30, you receive no interest on the sum withdrawn. It is therefore wise to make withdrawals after interest is paid, not before.

• *Be sure that all your savings are insured by a Federal or State agency, unless you know the management and are confident your money is safe.* Accounts in most savings associations and banks are insured for $10,000. If you have more than that sum in your account, it will not be insured.

It is possible, however, to have insured accounts for considerably more than that. Suppose a family consists of husband, wife and two children. The husband may have one account, the wife another and each child one as well. In addition, joint accounts can be insured: Husband and wife together, father and each child, mother and each child, and the two children together. Thus this family of four can have $100,000 in ten accounts, all fully covered by insurance.

• *Take advantage of special opportunities to increase your earning power.* Many institutions give "bonus dividends" of perhaps half of one percent on savings remaining in an account a year or longer. Over a period of time, these "bonus dividends" can add greatly to your capital.

Some savings and loan associations, for example, pay a "bonus" of ¼ to ½% over the regular dividends on savings units of $1,000 each which remain intact for a certain minimum number of years.

To encourage increased savings, some institutions offer valuable premiums—clocks, books, pens, etc.—for depositors who increase their savings by specified amounts and keep them intact for specified periods. Such offers often provide a substantial extra dividend in addition to those which the institution pays regularly.

How You Can Save Money in a Hurry

Even if you have an automatic savings program which takes a part of your income each pay day, you probably would occasionally like to save up for a particular purpose. Suppose you want to splurge on a dress or suit outside your normal budget allowance. Here are three tested ways to accumulate the money:

• *Concentrate on one coin only.* Every time you receive a certain coin (penny, nickel, dime, quarter) in change, put it aside. Do not use it until you have the sum you want.

Does this method work? Helen White, executive secretary of the National Thrift Committee, began to save pennies twenty years ago. Since then, she says, she has "never spent a cent." She has saved as much as $150 a year in this way.

• *Concentrate on one sacrifice only.* For example, wash and iron your laundry instead of having it done at a commercial laundry, and put the savings aside. Or try giving up desserts, restaurant meals, or movies until you reach your goal. A chain smoker gave up cigarettes and saved $3 a week.

• *Go all-out for a short time.* A young couple in northern Illinois decided to visit Chicago for a week-end to see sights they had heard about all their lives. Such a trip would cost more than they could normally afford. Since they were also putting money aside to buy a home, they did not wish to withdraw any savings to pay for it.

They decided upon an all-out effort to cut every-day expenses. The husband walked a mile and a quarter to work instead of taking the bus; he eliminated his morning coffee-break and carried his lunch instead of buying it downtown. His wife gave herself a home permanent and prepared stews and casseroles instead of chops and steaks. In one month, they saved $138—more than enough for a rousing week-end which made their sacrifice worthwhile.

These three methods employ a principle which makes any savings program effective. They use the automatic approach. Once you establish a routine, you can continue it as long as you care to—perhaps even indefinitely. Gradually you will lose the feeling that you are depriving yourself. The automatic approach succeeds because after a while you feel no pain as you accumulate spare cash.

chapter five

HOW TO PROTECT YOUR FAMILY WITH LIFE INSURANCE

Looking for financial peace of mind? It will be hard to find unless you have a good insurance program

A few years ago, two middle-aged fathers died within a month of each other in a suburb just outside Dallas, Texas. Both were home-owners. They each had two children. They earned about the same salaries and had about the same living standards.

The first man's wife and children still live in the same home, drive a new car, are fed and clothed as well as when he was still alive. But the second man's family was unable to pay its monthly bills and moved to a dingy flat in a run-down section. Now the widow works part-time to make ends meet.

Why the difference? Any youngster probably knows the answer: The first man had adequate life insurance while the second man did not. The odd part, however, is that both men spent about the same amount each month on their insurance programs. The first man's program did what it was supposed to do. The second man's was a make-shift affair and it failed the crucial test.

Americans are the most insurance-conscious people on earth. We have almost $500,000,000,000 worth of life insurance policies in force—almost one policy for every man, woman and child. Conscientious fathers make it a duty to leave their families provided for if they die. Most young couples also regard insurance as a necessity that should hold a top place in their financial planning.

Then why do cases like the one involving the second Texas family occur with clock-like regularity? The answer is that while Americans believe in the virtues of insurance, they often lack the information to decide which of many different policies is best for them, and how to obtain the best one at the lowest price. This chapter will give that information. Apply the principles you will find below, and you can be certain that your family will be financially secure if the main breadwinner dies or is disabled.

Many authorities have told me that the most important single fact to remember is that the breadwinner in your family probably already has life insurance through the Social Security program. Under this program of the federal government, employers, their employees, and self-employed people pay Social Security taxes during working years. These taxes go into special funds. When earnings stop because the worker retires, dies, or is disabled and is 50 years old or over, benefit payments are made to replace part of the earnings the family has lost. Thus Social Security occupies a vital part in your family financial planning. Here is what you should know about the insurance part of the program. The following information about your Social Security protection is provided by Victor Christgau, director of the Bureau of Old Age and Survivors' Insurance:

Nine out of ten working people are covered. If you have worked long enough to be covered, and if your work comes under the law, your family can get monthly payments if you die. In addition, a lump-sum payment of $255 or less can be made to your widow or widower living in the same household, or else it can be used to pay your burial expenses.

To be fully insured at the time of your death, you must have worked at least 1½ years at a job covered by Social

Security. This amount of work must have been done within the three years before your death. Once you have worked 10 years, your Social Security continues in force for life.

The amount of the payments your survivors get will depend upon the amount of work done and how much you earned. The amount of work is generally measured in "quarters of coverage"—roughly the 3-month periods beginning January 1, April 1, July 1, or October 1 of any year. For most kinds of employment, you get one quarter of coverage for each calendar quarter in which you earn $50 or more. If you are self-employed and have net earnings of $400 or more in a year, you get four quarters of coverage for that year. Earnings from self-employment of less than $400 a year do not count toward benefits. Farm workers get one quarter of coverage for each $100 of cash wages covered by the law paid in a year.

No matter how much you earn in any single quarter, you get four quarters of coverage for any year from 1951 through 1954 in which you earned $4,200 or more, and for any year since 1959 in which you earned $4,800 or more. But you can never get more than four quarters of coverage for any one year. You may have earned quarters of coverage by working in covered employment at any time after 1936 and in self-employment covered by the law after 1950.

Your "quarters on coverage" are used only in figuring whether you are insured—not in the amount of payments your survivors will get. This depends on your average earnings.

You will be fully insured at your death if at that time you have one quarter of coverage (earned at any time after 1936) for each three calendar quarters after 1950 and since you became 21 years old. You will never need more than 40 quarters of coverage to be fully insured for the payment of benefits to your widow and children while the children are unable to support themselves and for the payment of a lump sum death benefit. You will be "currently insured"—eligible for some but not all benefits—if you have at least six quarters of coverage within the three years before you die.

Your Social Security insurance payments can go to your unmarried children under 18; your children 18 or over if they were disabled before reaching 18 and have remained so since; your widow, of any age, if she is caring for a child entitled to payments; your widow at age 62 whether or not there is a child entitled to payments; your dependent widower at 65; your dependent parents (father 65, mother 62); your divorced wife if before your death, she was dependent upon you for her support pursuant to a court order or agreement, and if she has in her care your child who is also entitled to payments. For an aged widow or widower to get benefits, the marriage must have been in effect for at least one year.

Amount of Your Family's Benefits:

The monthly payment to your—	Is this part of your monthly amount [1]
Wife	One-half.
Child (when you have retired)	One-half.
Dependent husband	One-half.
Widow	Three-fourths.
Each child (after your death)	One-half (plus an additional one-fourth divided equally among all your children).
Dependent widower	Three-fourths.
Dependent parent	Three-fourths.

Some special reduction provisions are in effect for women workers and wives who elect to take their benefits between age 62 and 65.

How much work is required? Payments may be made to a widow with a child in her care, and to the child, if at the time of death the worker was either "fully insured" or "currently insured." Benefits for parents and widows aged 62 or over without children require a fully insured status; a widow-

---

[1] Except where dependents' or survivors' benefits must be reduced to keep the total family payments within the maximum provided in the law.

er's payments require both fully and currently insured status. The lump sum death benefit can be paid if you are either fully, or currently insured at your death.

Who Can Get Social Security Payments

This table shows for each type of social security benefit whether the worker must be fully insured, currently insured, or both.

Retirement Payments

Monthly payments to—	If you are—
You as a retired worker	Fully insured.
And monthly payments to your—	
Wife 62 or over	Fully insured.
Dependent child (under 18)	Fully insured.
Dependent child 18 or over who became totally disabled before that age	Fully insured.
Wife (regardless of age) if caring for child	Fully insured.
Dependent husband 65 or over	Both fully and currently insured.

Survivors Payments

Monthly payments to your—	If at death you are—
Widow 62 or over	Fully insured.
Widow or dependent divorced wife (regardless of age) if caring for your child who is entitled to benefits	Either fully or currently insured.
Dependent child (under 18)	Either fully or currently insured.
Dependent child 18 or over who became disabled before that age	Either fully or currently insured.
Dependent widower 65 or over	Both fully and currently insured.
Dependent parent (mother 62 or father 65)	Fully insured.
Lump-sum payment to your—	
Widow or widower, if living with you in the same household, or if he or she paid your burial expenses. Otherwise, the lump-sum can go to the person who paid your burial expenses	Either fully or currently insured.

Disability Payments

Monthly payments to—	If you are fully insured and have—
You and your dependents when you are aged 50-64 if you are totally disabled for work	20 quarters of coverage in the 40 calendar quarters before the beginning date of your disability.

What Do You Want Life Insurance to Do for You?

Social Security payments will provide for a minimum subsistence for your survivors if you die. It was intended to keep them from actual need—not to give them all the things you probably would want them to have.

Life insurance will help complete your program. It will give specific protection for your own individual circumstances. Your family situation, age, earning prospects, your ability to save money if nobody forces you to—in all these conditions you differ from your neighbors. Unlike Social Security, which provides the same basic, minimum security for all, life insurance policies can help you achieve individual ambitions. For instance:

Dave Loomis is 25, married with three children. He owns a textile business which he thinks has a great future. He wants to use all his cash to expand the business, but also wishes to protect his family fully if he dies. His objective: Maximum insurance now at minimum cost.

Al McKay is 26, a salesman with two youngsters. This year he landed four huge accounts and his earnings will triple last year's. But Al fears that next year business will fall off sharply. He wants to buy a lot of insurance while he has plenty of money—and he wants it to remain in force even if he has several poor years and can't pay any premiums.

Frank Powell, a grocery store clerk, seeks protection for his youngsters and security in his old age. He finds it difficult to save and nibbles away his paycheck on non-essential items every time. He wants to be forced to pay a certain amount out of his salary each month.

Ben Talmadge has just bought a new home with a $20,000 mortgage. He fears that if he died, his wife would be forced to sell quickly, taking the first offer she received. He wants insurance that would pay off the mortgage in full upon his death.

All these persons can buy policies tailored to their personal needs. In fact, insurance men boast that no matter what your particular requirements, there is a policy to fit them.

In evaluating your own family's needs, officials of the Institute of Life Insurance told me, you might keep in mind answers to these three questions:

1. Whose Lives Should Be Insured? Most families would feel real financial need only if the chief breadwinner died. Of course, the death of any family member would be a shock and funeral expenses might be difficult to pay, but the main income would continue. Real financial tragedies happen when the family income is cut off—and there is little or no insurance money to replace it.

Experts agree that if the father is the sole support, most or all the insurance should be on his life. If the family depends upon the wages of the wife or children, they should also be insured in proportion to the support they provide. Many young families also add a policy on the wife's life. While no one could replace a mother in the home, such a policy would provide funds for skilled help to keep the family going, for a time at least.

2. How Much Insurance Should You Carry? The amount of insurance most people carry generally depends as much upon their income as upon the amount of protection they actually need. Some studies have shown that the typical American family puts aside three percent of its income for life insurance

—that the man who earns $150 a week will set aside $4.50 of it in this way.

The percentage of your income that you should devote to insurance will depend first upon earning capacity. A man who must support a family of five on $70 a week will naturally be unable to apply as high a percentage as will the man earning $500 a week.

In addition, your needs will vary at different stages of your life. The young married man with small children will need a great deal. A middle-aged man with grown youngsters may need less. An elderly man sees the cycle after a full turn: He may keep some of his policies to protect his wife and turn the rest into income.

If you have a low income and young dependents, you may be unable to provide as much insurance as conditions might warrant. In that case, it may be advisable to buy the maximum protection and to defer "cash value" insurance until later, or to consider combining term and permanent insurance.

But don't put so much into insurance that you lack money for other important things—for adequate food and shelter, the ordinary comforts of life, and a savings account for "rainy day" emergencies. One young couple became overly-conscientious about their insurance obligations. Although the father earns $97 a week, he spends $14 for insurance. His wife must shave food costs. Minor luxuries—a trip to a theater, dinner at a restaurant, a day at the beach—are impossible. Ironically, only if the father dies will the family be able to afford the things it denies itself while he is alive.

Generally, young families first try to have insurance adequate to keep the family going—in their own home, children in their usual schools—until they could work out a new arrangement. As income increases, they add to their program—to keep pace with increased family needs or for special family goals such as education.

As a minimum, strive to provide insurance equal to three

to five years' income. If you earn $5,000 a year, you would therefore want at least $15,000 worth of insurance.

3. Which Kind of Insurance Is Best for You? Basically, there are three kinds of policies:

TERM INSURANCE is pure protection—usually nothing else. It always has an expiration period when the protection runs out. While this might be only one year, it is usually five or ten years. However, you can obtain term policies which you can renew without taking an additional medical examination. For example, a common type five-year policy allows you to renew at the expiration date even if you have contracted a deadly disease in the meantime.

Premiums on each five-year policy are based upon your age when it is written. Thus the same amount of protection costs more and more the older you get. Moreover, most companies will not renew any term policies after you are 55 or 60.

Some policies are also convertible. Within prescribed periods, and without an additional medical examination, you can switch to a policy in which you have a cash value and which will continue in force throughout your lifetime. Premiums on such a policy per thousand dollars of insurance are of course higher.

Term insurance provides maximum protection at the lowest premium outlay. For instance, one company sells $1,000 worth of protection for five years to a man of 25 for about $6.75 per year. For a straight life policy for $1,000—one in which the cash value builds up gradually—his premium would be $15.50 per year. A term policy is often suggested for the young husband with small children and low earning power, to carry over until he is able to convert to permanent insurance.

Insurance agents may also recommend term insurance to persons needing protection for a limited period. An author began writing a novel which would take three years to finish. If he died in that time, all his work would be wasted. To protect his wife and children, he took a three-year term policy for $50,000. He reasoned that if he died thereafter, they would inherit royalties from his book.

STRAIGHT OR ORDINARY LIFE INSURANCE is permanent. Unlike term policies, on which premiums increase each time you renew, the premiums on straight life insurance remain the same all your life. They are the average of what you might be expected to pay at various ages of a normal life. Therefore, they are much higher than term insurance premiums when you are young, and much lower when you are older.

The extra amounts you pay in the early years of the policy create a cash value available to borrow if needed, or to take as cash or income should you decide to give up your policy.

The cash value has other possible uses. Suppose you can no longer pay your premiums. You can use it to pay in full for less insurance which will remain in force all your life. Or you can use your cash value to keep the policy effective for as many additional years and days as it will provide.

More ordinary life insurance policies are sold than any other kind. They have many variations. One of these is the limited payment policy, which remains in effect for a lifetime although you pay premiums only for a stipulated period—for 10, 15 or 20 years, or until you reach age 60 or 65. Premiums for such policies are naturally higher than those on which you must pay for longer periods. Also, the cash values build more quickly.

Limited payment policies are usually recommended to persons with high incomes now who may not remain in those brackets. Typical purchasers: Big league baseball players who may never earn a five-figure salary once they hang up their spikes; popular singers now riding the crest of a fad; or anyone who wishes to telescope premiums into a specific number of years.

ENDOWMENT INSURANCE. This emphasizes savings features more than protection. Endowment policies are also written for specified periods, often 10 or 20 years. At the end of the period, you may take the full amount of the policy in cash or as income. The premium rates per thousand are higher than for any other policy. As a result, cash values build rapidly.

Some popular policies combine straight life with term or with endowment insurance, or term with endowment, or even all three types together.

For example, "Family Plan" policies offer some coverage for every member of the family. A typical plan provides: Straight life insurance of $5,000 for the husband; term insurance for his wife of about $1,000 (more if she is younger than he, less if she is older); and term insurance of $1,000 for each child. At age 21, this can be converted to $5,000 permanent insurance without another medical examination. Otherwise, it expires at that age.

Premiums on a "Family Plan" policy become paid in full if the breadwinner dies. This type of policy will insure all the children alive when the policy is written, and also, without extra charge, any children born thereafter.

A "Family Plan" policy generally will cost less than the same amount of insurance written for the husband and wife alone.

"Family Income" policies also combine straight life with term insurance. The term policy may be at a fixed premium, with the amount of coverage decreasing as the insured gets older. These policies are based on the theory that the average family needs less protection as the breadwinner ages and the children approach the time when they can support themselves.

These policies are often sold to homeowners. The amount of the term insurance corresponds to their mortgage. The face amount of the term policy decreases yearly and so does their mortgage debt as they pay off part of the principal. Such policies guarantee that an insured man's wife and children will own the home free and clear if he dies.

Another variation provides for equal amounts of ordinary life insurance and term insurance when the policy is written. The amount of the term coverage decreases each year until the end of a certain period, generally from 19 to 25 years, when it stops entirely. If the insured dies before the policy expires, his dependents will receive a specified amount monthly until the expiration date. Then they receive the full proceeds of the ordinary life insurance policy.

Suppose a man wishes to make sure that his son can afford a college education fifteen years from now. The father takes out a "family income policy" with 15-year term insurance. But he dies after three years. The insurance company pays a stipulated amount each month until the boy reaches 21. Then it pays the amount of the ordinary life policy to the beneficiary.

There are literally hundreds of other insurance plans. All emphasize some special type of coverage which may—or may not—be suitable for you. In addition, many "riders" can be written into almost any policy. The most common are:

DOUBLE INDEMNITY. This provides that your beneficiary will receive double the face value if you die an accidental death. The cost of this rider is slight. However, some authorities question its worth. They argue that the survivors generally need no more money when a breadwinner dies accidentally than if he dies a natural death. In fact, the opposite might be true. The survivor might be able to collect damage from the person responsible for the accident, while in the case of a lingering illness, high medical and hospital bills might cut deeply into the insurance benefits.

DISABILITY INCOME. Also available for an extra premium, this will give you a specified income if you become totally disabled—suffer the loss of eyesight or the use of both hands or arms, for example.

DISABILITY WAIVER OF PREMIUM. This stipulates that your insurance will become full paid-up if you become totally disabled and thus lose your earning power. Many experts recommend this relatively inexpensive extra because it would mean continuing to have your insurance program intact when most needed.

SETTLEMENT OPTIONS. At no extra cost, most policies provide that the insured or the beneficiary may stipulate how the insurance money is to be paid. Generally, you have four choices:

1. Take the full amount in one sum.
2. Leave the money with the insurance company until needed, meantime receiving interest as stipulated in the policy.
3. Take guaranteed income—so much per month, or income for a certain length of time.
4. Take monthly income for life.

Incidentally, it's always a good idea to name a second person (contingent) in case the first beneficiary is not living.

These same options are usually available to the policyholder himself when he wishes to give up protection and take the cash values in his policies.

WHAT $10,000 WILL PROVIDE UNDER THE FOUR SETTLEMENT OPTIONS [*]

Option	Settlement
INTEREST OPTION Money left at interest until the family asks for it.	At 2½% interest, $250 a year until the money is withdrawn.
AMOUNT OPTION A regular income of as much money as you want, paid until money and interest are used up.	$100 a month for 9 years and 3 months, for example, or $200 a month for 4 years and 4 months.

TIME OPTION
A monthly income to last as many years as you want, paid until money and interest are used up.

10 years' income of $92 a month, for example, or 20 years' income of $51 a month.

LIFETIME INCOME OPTION
A regular income guaranteed for the person's lifetime.

$50 a month for life (for a woman 65 years old)
$65 a month for life (for a man 65 years old)

---

* Interest figured at the guaranteed rate of 2½%. Companies will pay higher interest than this as earned.

—Source: Institute of Life Insurance

Where You Can Buy Insurance

Where you obtain your policies may make the difference between a program which will be easy to handle and which will provide adequate protection, and one which could burden you while you live and yet give an inadequate sum to your beneficiary upon your death.

There are three main sources of insurance policies:

GROUP INSURANCE. As its name applies, this type is usually available to numbers of persons with something in common—employees in the same company, members of a union or fraternal organization, even members of any club. It is usually term insurance and has no cash value.

Many companies will issue policies to members of any group large enough to be a fairly representative cross section of the general population. In that way they will be sure that they do not get too many poor risks—people who will die at a younger age than the average.

Premium rates are figured on the average ages of all members. Then the same rate is charged to all, regardless of age. This means that older members often pay less than half what they would pay for individual policies elsewhere. However, even the rates paid by younger members are lower than they would be outside the group.

Generally no medical examination is required when a large number of persons are insured in a group. Persons who might be refused insurance elsewhere because of poor health, or who might have to pay extra premiums, can obtain the same protection at the same price as everyone else. When they leave the group, they usually can convert to ordinary life policies without a medical examination.

Group insurance is such a bargain that most authorities agree that it should be bought by everyone who can do so.

G.I. Insurance, or national service life insurance, is a form of group insurance. The government handles the program and pays the administration costs from taxes. Consequently, premium rates are extremely low. Other provisions—cash values, the right to switch from one policy to another and the right to renew a policy at low cost after it has lapsed—are exceptionally liberal. This insurance is available only to members of the armed forces.

CONVENTIONAL LIFE INSURANCE COMPANIES. There are an estimated 600 life insurance companies in the United States. Most offer a complete selection of basic policies plus many special-feature policies to meet individual requirements. Therefore it is difficult, if not impossible, for the average person to select the company which offers the best rate on the policy which is best for him. As a practical matter, therefore, you should choose a reliable company with an unblemished reputation—or an insurance agent with the same.

If possible, choose an agent who has the experience to answer your questions intelligently, to design an insurance program specifically for you, and who has served your friends or acquaintances satisfactorily. Avoid the high-pressure type who is determined to sell costly policies without regard for your own desires. Remember that in addition to providing protection in case you die, an insurance policy should give you a sense of security while you live.

From any agent you have a right to expect a well thought-out program which is within your ability to pay and which will give you protection where and when you need it. To prepare such a program, your agent must know certain personal facts about you—your age, income, your other assets such as savings accounts, real estate possessions, etc. You will make it difficult or impossible to serve you properly if you withhold the information he needs to custom-tailor a program to your needs.

Take your time before deciding upon any policy. Once you sign up for one it may be costly to discontinue if it does not fulfill your needs later. If you are still young, you will probably buy additional policies as your earning power increases. These should build on, rather than supplant, the policies you bought earlier.

If you do not understand any provisions in the policies, ask the agent to explain them. Do not be satisfied until you understand thoroughly.

If you know what kind of policy you want, you might examine the rates of several companies. You should be certain, however, to compare premiums for identical policies. One policy may contain provisions—such as the right to convert term insurance—which might be worth the additional cost.

In comparing rates, you will also have to understand what dividends you can expect. This subject often confuses the public, because there are two kinds of company: Mutual companies and stock companies. In effect, the policyholders themselves own the mutual companies. They are entitled to receive any sums above those necessary to pay death benefits, administration and sales costs, and to build up reserves in case of a sudden increase in deaths. These extra amounts are returned to them in the form of dividends. However, mutual companies cannot estimate exactly how much they will pay out in benefits each year, nor even what their other costs will be. Therefore they tend to charge higher premiums than may be necessary and return the excess to the policyholders in the form of dividends.

A mutual company can tell from past experience what its cost will be, but cannot guarantee them. And while it may expect to pay a certain dividend, it is not obliged to do so if its costs are higher than it has anticipated. So while you can be reasonably sure of getting the promised dividends from a mutual company, you do not have a complete guarantee. Insurance sold by mutual companies is called the "participating" type because policyholders participate in the profits, if any.

Stock companies are *non-participating:* Their profits are returned to the private owners—the stockholders—and not the policyholders. These companies guarantee the dividends they will pay. If they pay out more than they take in, the stockholders suffer. Non-participating companies often sell policies at lower premium rates than do mutual companies. However, mutual policies may be less expensive when their dividends are subtracted from the premiums.

Not many years ago, most insurance company revenues came from "industrial" policies. These had face values of as little as a hundred dollars, and the premiums sometimes amounted to only 25 cents a month. They were collected by agents who went from door to door. Proceeds from such policies often even failed to cover the burial expenses of the insured.

This type of insurance is still sold, although to a lesser extent than formerly. It is more expensive than other types because you must pay the costs of regular visits by the collector —a substantial factor. Moreover, insurance companies have found that buyers of industrial policies have shorter life spans than purchasers of ordinary life policies, and premium rates reflect this experience. As a result of these factors, it has been estimated that you can get $3,000 worth of protection in an ordinary life policy for the sum that would buy only $2,000 worth with an industrial policy.

SAVINGS BANK LIFE INSURANCE. Clyde S. Casady, executive vice-president of the Savings Banks Association of Massachusetts, states that around the turn of the century, almost all life insurance was sold by high-pressure salesmen. High selling expenses and excessive lapses resulted in policyholders paying more for protection than was justified. Louis Brandeis, later to become Justice of the United States Supreme Court, began advocating a type of "supermarket insurance"—the kind men and women could buy over the counter and avoid high pressure salesmanship and selling costs.

This kind of insurance was first sold by savings banks in

WHAT VARIOUS POLICIES COST
Approximate Annual Premiums for $1,000 of Insurance *

Type of Policy	Age at Which Policy is Issued					
	20	21	22	23	24	25
Five Year Term (Renewable and convertible)	$ 5.65	$ 5.70	$ 5.80	$ 5.90	$ 6.00	$ 6.10
Ten Year Term (Renewable and convertible)	6.80	6.90	7.00	7.10	7.20	7.30
Straight Life	14.15	14.50	14.85	15.25	15.65	16.10
Life-Paid-Up-at-65	16.20	16.60	17.10	17.60	18.15	18.70
20 Payment Life	25.85	26.30	26.75	27.25	27.75	28.30
Retirement Income at 65 (Male)	25.50	26.30	27.15	28.05	29.05	30.15
20 Year Endowment	46.95	47.00	47.05	47.10	47.15	47.20

—Source: Institute of Life Insurance.

* Rates shown are approximate premium rates for life insurance protection. Rates of "participating" policies would be slightly higher but the cost would be lowered by annual dividends. "Non-participating" policy premium rates would be somewhat lower than those shown, and no dividends would be paid.

Massachusetts in 1907. The Massachusetts legislature provided that there were to be no outside salesmen to solicit business. In 1938, New York permitted savings banks to sell insurance, and Connecticut also followed suit in 1941.

Savings banks may sell insurance only to residents in their own state. They do not offer the wide variety of plans sold by most insurance companies. However, they sell the basic types—term, ordinary life, limited payment, endowment and group insurance as well as certain other special policies.

Six Points to Remember

• *You may—or may not—get a bargain by buying life insurance by mail.* Victor H. Nyborg, president of the Association of Better Business Bureaus, says that before you do so, you should thoroughly investigate the company, establish beyond doubt that it is licensed to do business in your state, and make certain that it is reliable and has a good record of performance.

Some fly-by-night companies attract customers by mail. When the time comes for them to pay off, they may point to clauses in their policies which enable them to avoid paying what you have expected to get. Conducting business by mail is not as inexpensive as many people imagine. Therefore a company which offers "bargain rates" unobtainable elsewhere should be regarded with suspicion. Be sure to read and understand the policy before buying it, and carefully note the exceptions or exemptions. Otherwise you may discover later that you do not have the protection you thought you were getting.

Some firms which write policies only for "good medical risks" may offer bona-fide bargains, however. For example, some companies sell policies at special rates to clergymen, who generally lead healthier, less dangerous lives than other persons and thus have longer life spans on the average. Even in the case of specialty companies, however, it pays to double-check their references.

- *Find out whether you can choose to pay premiums on a yearly, semi-annual or quarterly basis.* There may be a substantial difference in cost between one annual payment and four quarterly ones. If you intend to take out a large amount of insurance, you may be able to pay for it on a quarterly—even a monthly basis—without extra cost. Here is how:

Most companies write insurance in thousand-dollar units. You pay the same premium per thousand whether you buy a policy for $1,000, or for $10,000. Instead of buying one policy with an annual premium, you might buy several policies with each annual premium staggered several months apart. You will get the same protection as if you took out one policy for a large sum, but you can pay in quarterly installments at no extra cost.

- *Keep your policies in a safe place.* Your survivors should be familiar with the terms of the policies and should know what options are open. They should also know where the policies are kept. (Safe deposit boxes may be sealed by law upon the death of their owner, and may not be opened except upon a court order. This may take time and may prove inconvenient if the beneficiary needs proceeds to pay funeral and other immediate expenses.)

- *Make sure you know the special provisions of your policy.* Most companies allow a period of grace (usually 31 days) after the premium payment is due. Your policy will remain in force during this time even if your payment is delayed. If your policy has an automatic premium loan provision, the premium will be automatically paid by a policy loan if you do not make your payment within the grace period.

- *Once you start an insurance policy, be prepared to continue it.* A large part of your early premiums will be devoted to sales commissions and other insurance company expenses. Not so much will be devoted to building a cash reserve. If you change your mind and drop a policy after it has run a short while, much of what you have paid will have been eaten up.

Even a policy which now may not be best for your changed needs might be worth keeping if you have already paid one year's premium. That is when its value to you will increase.

• *There is no way of making sure that you choose the best policy.* You could do so only if you could foretell the future. The young man who buys only term insurance and dies soon thereafter has made the wisest possible decision. If he holds term insurance all his life and lives to his nineties, his program was perhaps the poorest he could have devised. A thirty-year-old man who buys an endowment policy may have been wise if he lives to be seventy, but unwise if he dies at thirty-one.

You will not know how you should have played the game until it is all over. So what should you do now?

Just act on the principle that the best insurance program is one that eases your mind. It should give you the assurance that you have provided for your family as well as you can. You cannot do more.

chapter six

COULD YOUR LIFE BE RUINED IN TWENTY SECONDS?

It could—if you did not protect yourself against damage suits which happen every day

In addition to life insurance, you will need other protection against an unforeseen accident or illness which could deal a crippling financial blow from which you might never recover. Here are the various kinds of insurance to consider.

Automobile Insurance

Automobile insurance that protects you in case you injure someone else or damage his property is the most important to have. You flirt with financial ruin if you do not carry such insurance. Suppose you are driving slowly along a street. A man suddenly steps between two parked cars and into your path. You cannot stop in time and he is killed. Although you are really blameless, his widow sues you and a jury awards her $100,000 to compensate for the loss of her husband's support. If you are not insured for that amount, all you own—your home, car, savings—may be seized to pay the judgment.

Such cases have happened. So even if you are a supercautious driver, your own peace of mind requires that you have insurance backed by a company which will defend your interests.

I asked J. Carroll Bateman, general manager of the Insurance Information Institute, to describe the basic coverage car owners should have. He outlines four kinds of policy you can get:

LIABILITY INSURANCE. This is the kind which is mandatory in three states and which is also most important to have. It protects you against claims made by other persons, if the accident is your fault. Consider these possibilities: Your car runs into another, smashing its radiator and fender. You strike a pedestrian, breaking his leg. You drive into a fence and knock it down. While parking, you scrape the fender of another car. In all these cases, a liability policy will protect you. Your insurance company will pay claims, up to the limits of your policy, if you were at fault, and it also will defend you against law suits brought against you by the other persons involved in the accident.

You should have at least enough protection to meet the requirements of the financial or safety responsibility law of your state, or the compulsory law if you live in New York, North Carolina or Massachusetts. (The Massachusetts law requires only bodily injury liability insurance, not property damage liability.) Generally speaking, safety or financial responsibility laws require motorists who have been in accidents involving death, injury or property damage over a specified amount such as $50 to show evidence that they are able to pay for the damage they caused. A valid insurance policy in the proper limits constitutes acceptable evidence, or cash or certain bonds may be posted.

The laws of the states vary as to the amount of protection required. The requirements range from limits of $5,000 to $20,000 to be paid to one person for bodily injury or death, and from $10,000 to $30,000 to be paid to more than one person injured or killed in the same accident. The requirements for coverage against claims for damage to property range from $1,000 to $5,000.

Remember, these are the minimum amounts of protection. You can, for example, get bodily injury liability protection in amounts up to $100,000 and $300,000, and even higher.

Rates for liability insurance have risen steadily, due to increases in accidents and the liberality of juries in handing out fantastic sums for injuries. Everybody seems to be claim-conscious—a good reason why you are highly vulnerable if you do not carry enough liability coverage.

MEDICAL PAYMENTS INSURANCE. If you or a passenger are injured in an accident while in your car, this kind of insurance would pay for medical expenses, including such items as ambulance service. This protection usually is purchased in amounts ranging from $500 to $5,000. It also affords protection to you and relatives living in your household for injuries resulting from an accident while in an automobile, entering or leaving one, or by being struck by an automobile. This coverage differs from automobile liability insurance in that it applies regardless of whether you were at fault in the accident. It is relatively inexpensive and encourages instantaneous medical attention, thereby often enabling doctors to treat cases before they can grow into major conditions.

FAMILY PROTECTION COVERAGE. This will cover you if you are injured by a hit-and-run driver, or by an uninsured motorist. It also is relatively inexpensive.

COMPREHENSIVE INSURANCE. This will compensate you directly if your car is stolen or damaged by fire, floods, or many other causes except collision or upset.

COLLISION INSURANCE. Under such a policy, the insurance company will pay up to the limits of the policy all but a specified amount of your repair bills if your car has been in an accident—even if you were the responsible party. Usual policies carry $50 or $100 deductible clauses, meaning that the insurer will pay for damages over those amounts, up to the actual cash value of your car.

Suppose your car and another collide and it is difficult to place the blame. Your insurer will pay for repairs to your car (in excess of the specified amount deducted). Then it will try to recover the damages from the other party, if it is established that the other party was at fault. Whether it collects or not, you will be compensated.

If you must save on car insurance costs, you might consider a higher deductible on your collision coverage. The protection it provides is not nearly so essential for your financial security as liability and medical payment insurance. If the worst happened and your car was a total wreck, its value would be the most you could lose. While substantial, this loss would be nothing like that if you ran into another car, killed several people, and faced damage suits totaling many thousands of dollars. However, you may be required to carry collision insurance if you buy the car on borrowed money, for the lender may want his protection for his loan.

What will automobile insurance cost? Rates vary greatly, depending upon:

• *Where you live.* Rates usually are higher in big cities, relatively low in smaller communities or rural areas.

• *What use you make of the car.* One driven for business purposes requires a higher premium than one used solely for pleasure. Underwriters know that business cars are driven longer and more often, hence are in more accidents.

• *Age of drivers.* A family with a male driver under 25 must pay higher premiums—in some cases double the regular premium—because accident frequency and severity among such drivers are extremely high. Some companies prefer not to write a new policy for a family with an unmarried male driver under 25.

• *Your previous accident records.* If you have been responsible for several accidents within a short period, your premiums may be increased in some states the next time you seek to renew your insurance. Some companies offer lower rates to drivers who have a good driving record.

• *Original value of your car or its present market value.* A new Cadillac obviously costs more to replace than a five-year old Chevrolet. Comprehensive and collision insurance rates reflect this difference.

Home and Personal Property Insurance

You will probably invest several thousand dollars in your home and its furnishings. The savings and loan association or other institution which holds your mortgage will require enough insurance to protect its investment in case of fire or other damage. You should also protect your own investment.

The Insurance Information Institute says you need a minimum of two kinds: Dwelling insurance to cover losses if your house is damaged or destroyed by fire, lightning or other specified hazards; and contents insurance to cover losses if your furnishings and other possessions are destroyed or stolen.

Other kinds of insurance are needed to provide protection against common hazards. These kinds have been "packaged" with standard fire insurance to provide comprehensive protection under what usually is called a "homeowners" policy. They afford broad protection at a lower cost than the premium for the various kinds of coverage if purchased separately.

DWELLING INSURANCE. Insurance companies sell policies which protect you only in case of fire or lightning, but you should have extended coverage. This gives protection if the house is damaged by windstorm, hail, smoke and smudge, riot and explosion, and in the event of contingencies with a greater chance of happening than many imagine—for example, a plane crashing onto your property or a car careening over your lawn and into your house. This extended coverage is available with a $50 deductible at a greatly reduced price.

For a slight extra charge, you can buy protection against vandalism—for instance, against Halloween pranks which might cause hundreds of dollars damage. Against vehicle damage—if, for instance, you accidentally plow through the back of your garage. Against some forms of water damage—if water spills out of the bathtub and ruins your carpeting, for example. (Water damage must result from internal sources such as plumbing or appliances. Water damage from sources such as seepage, backing up of sewers and floods is not covered.) Against falling objects, such as large branches crashing through your roof.

You can also get a rider to your dwelling insurance policy which guarantees to pay a specified portion of your additional living expenses away from home if you are forced to leave it because a fire, explosion, or other specified accident has made it uninhabitable.

PERSONAL PROPERTY INSURANCE. This covers possessions both in and away from your home—your furniture, appliances, clothing, sports equipment, etc. For a small extra charge, it can protect them against theft away from home as well. You should have this coverage whether you own a home or rent.

On losses away from home, a typical policy will pay up to 10 percent of the total insurance. Suppose you insured your home's contents for $1,000 and fire damages your fishing rods, camera and golf clubs while on vacation. You could collect only up to $100 for the loss.

To get maximum protection from your personal property insurance, you should accurately estimate what your home's contents are worth. Go from room to room. List all your possessions with their original costs, date and place of purchase, and probable replacement cost today. This record will give you a clear idea of the value of your possessions and will help you if you ever file a damage claim.

Personal Liability Insurance

A personal liability policy will protect you against an almost unbelievable number of accidents for which you might be held responsible. Consider these examples:

A milkman tripped over a loose brick on the front steps of a house, fractured his skull, and could not work for months. He sued the homeowner for $3,000 in medical bills, for $2,000 to cover his lost wages, and for $25,000 to compensate him for the permanent injury he suffered.

Playing baseball, a boy swung his bat and hit another boy's arm, fracturing his wrist. Medical bills totalled $300, and the injured boy's parents sued the other boy's parents.

A family piled old lumber in the yard to use as firewood. A neighbor's boy ran into the yard uninvited, slipped on a nail, gashed his arm and contracted blood poisoning. His parents sued, claiming the owner had maintained an "attractive nuisance" which lured their boy to play.

In examples like these, you could be held legally responsible. You might be forced to pay substantial damages. You could even be wiped out financially.

A personal liability policy will protect you against suits resulting from accidents on your own premises and will also cover you and your family away from home. For instance, if you are playing golf and your ball accidentally injures another golfer, you will be defended against damages. This broad coverage makes a personal liability policy desirable for all families, whether they own homes or not.

What will it cost? The cost of fire insurance on a home of plain common construction that is not exposed to any extra hazard will range from 60 cents to $2.00 per year for each $1,000 of coverage, says the Insurance Information Institute. Extended coverage insurance costs range from $1.50 to $3.50 per $1,000. Personal property rates are about the same. About

$1.00 per year will give you $1,000 worth of personal liability coverage.

You can save substantially by buying a package policy which combines home, personal property and personal liability insurance. Because selling, bookkeeping and administrative expenses are lower, you can get this blanket coverage for up to 20 percent less than the policies would cost if bought separately.

Title Insurance

When you buy a home or other real estate, you face a possibility that a controversy over its ownership may arise later and your legal rights may be questioned. The reason: All land has a history going back hundreds of years. The plot you buy may have changed hands dozens of times. In any of those transactions, someone who did not legally possess the property might have sold it nevertheless. Or perhaps the seller was under age and could not legally make a contract. Maybe he was mentally incompetent or was drunk at the time—hence, could not make a valid agreement. If so, the original owner's heirs might claim the property and sue to take it from you.

These are remote possibilities—but they happen. Title insurance was created to protect property owners against the danger that they might lose their property in that way. If you have a policy, the insurance company will contest all claims.

Costs of title insurance vary. In one instance it costs $60 for the first $10,000 of coverage and $3 for each thousand additional. If you buy a mortgaged house, you may be obliged to take this insurance to protect the mortgage-holder's investment. Make sure you take out enough insurance to protect your investment as well.

This insurance remains in force as long as you hold the property. When a new owner takes over, a new policy will be required.

The lawyer who represents you when you buy property, or the institution which holds your mortgage, will suggest a title insurance company.

Hospital and Health Insurance

A generation ago, the family that saw one of its members carried to a hospital could often expect hard financial times—perhaps years of struggling to pay the hospital bills involved along with the doctors' fees. Today a trip to a hospital is not, for most families, the major financial catastrophe it once was. Within the past generation, hospital insurance has become the rule rather than the exception. Spokesmen for the American Medical Association say that two-thirds of all Americans are now covered by hospital or health insurance, or both, through one of the many programs now available in the United States.

These basic kinds of protection are available:

HOSPITALIZATION INSURANCE. Under the Blue Cross Plan—the so-called "Hospitals' plan" which has the greatest number of subscribers—the insured person may stay at a semi-private hospital room for a specified number of days without cost. A percentage of his hospital bill for longer periods is also paid. He may be entitled to laboratory tests, x-ray examinations and other services at no extra cost.

Blue Cross and similar hospital and health insurance plans are often sold to employers as a "fringe benefit" for employees. The employer may pay each premium or deduct it from their pay checks, but they may maintain their membership if they change jobs. Then they may pay the premiums themselves on a quarterly, semi-annual or annual basis.

Blue Cross authorities say that the more typical pattern is for the employer to deduct the premiums from the employees' pay each month. The insured person receives a membership card, entitling him and members of his family (wife and children under nineteen years of age) to receive hospital care for periods up to 120 days per year, plus other hospital services. Under most Blue Cross plans, you cannot receive treatments for an injury or illness if that illness or injury is already covered by the Workmen's Compensation Law, or if you are entitled to receive it in a Veteran's Hospital.

Individuals not eligible to be enrolled as members of a group may enroll under an individual payment policy during special recruiting periods held several times a year.

"DOCTOR BILL" INSURANCE. The most popular of these is Blue Shield, a non-profit program, like Blue Cross. It covers surgical and medical expenses in specified amounts. This insurance lists a wide variety of services for which it will pay your doctor, including some he performs in his office. Blue Shield and Blue Cross plans are sometimes available from the same management.

In some areas, a doctor participating in this plan agrees to accept specified payments for his services if your family's income does not exceed a certain amount—say $6,000. If your earnings are greater, he can charge more. The insurance company then pays the specified amount and you pay the remainder.

Doctor bill plans are generally bought by groups. But individuals may continue them if they leave the place where they were enrolled.

MAJOR MEDICAL EXPENSE INSURANCE. This type can be obtained from private insurance companies. Unlike Blue Cross or Blue Shield, they pay you in cash if you have certain specified conditions requiring medical treatment in or out of a hospital.

These policies usually carry a deductible provision. They will pay all expenses over a certain amount—for example, $300 or $500. If you have a policy with a high deductible provision, you will have to pay small medical bills but will be protected against big expenses resulting from serious and prolonged illnesses.

You can be protected (for a price) against the costs of every kind of treatment by a licensed physician anywhere. Also covered are charges for a licensed nurse when one is necessary, ambulance costs, surgical appliances and drug bills. The total amount of expenses paid by a major medical policy vary. Some companies pay a maximum of $5,000; others go to $10,000 or more. You choose—and pay accordingly—for the coverage you want.

LOSS-OF-INCOME INSURANCE. This is mainly designed for professional men, self-employed persons such as shopowners, and employees whose salary would be discontinued if they contracted a long illness and could not work.

Under a typical policy, you must have one week's illness, attested to by a physician, before you can claim payments. This provision prevents excessive payments due to colds and similar minor ailments. After the waiting period, you will receive a certain amount every week for one year, and a lesser amount each week for the following year, after which the payments stop. Other policies require waiting periods of several weeks, even three months. Some make payments for only one year; others might continue them longer, even for a lifetime disability. Obviously, the more liberal the payments you will get, the higher the premiums you must pay.

If you seek protection against drawn-out, crippling illness, and yet wish to keep premium rates low, you might choose a policy that pays off only after several weeks have elapsed. Increasing the waiting time on a loss-of-income policy is like increasing the deductible provision on an automobile collision policy.

Beware of These Trick Clauses in Your Health Policy

Some "bargain" accident and health insurance policies contain clauses which may make them highly unsuitable. Among them are:

A clause giving the company the right to cancel the policy at any time. Naturally, as long as you are profitable to the company, it will not cancel your policy. But this clause would allow it to cancel when you might need protection most—during a long, serious, or recurrent illness, for example.

"This policy may be renewed WITH THE CONSENT OF THE COMPANY from term to term . . ." If the company refuses to "consent," your policy is no better than one which can be cancelled. Some of these policies are sold with quarterly premiums, permitting the company to drop you after any three-month period.

"Falsity of any statement in the application for this policy . . . shall bar all right to recover." You will be held responsible even for any honest inaccuracies and omissions. A policy even ten or fifteen years old may be declared null and void by the courts just when you vitally need its protection. Thus you may pay premiums for years for protection that does not exist. Many companies agree that after a policy has been in force for two years, they will guarantee its validity. This gives you greater protection.

Clause which refers to "bodily injury sustained through accidental means." The company is not liable for injuries resulting from normal acts such as moving a desk, opening a window or swinging a golf club. It can claim that the "means" in each case was an intended act, not accidental. Since nearly half of all injuries involve no accidental means, this clause could cut your protection in half.

Total Disability clause which describes "total disability" as "inability to engage in ANY occupation or employment." You might be disabled from performing your usual work and still be denied any payments, because you could conceivably perform other duties or tasks.

Continuous Disability clause like "if said injury (or sickness) shall wholly and CONTINUOUSLY disable the insured . . ." Wording like this signifies that if you are disabled, get well and then suffer a relapse, your second period of disability will not be covered. This is a serious limitation because frequently people in poor health are up and down several times before long illness sets in.

Clause stating you must be confined to your house to obtain benefits. Many sicknesses have short, acute stages, followed by long periods when you must "take it easy." Heart diseases and pneumonia are common causes of disability of this type. Recuperative periods often last for months, during which you should get fresh air and sunshine. But under a house-confining clause, you would not be compensated if you went out of doors onto porches, hospital grounds or parks.

Lack of Grace Clause, such as one stating "This policy may be renewed by payment of the premium ON OR BEFORE DUE DATE." This wording means that if you pay your premium even one day after it is due, the company may refuse to accept it and the policy will be out of existence. You might be out of town when your premium falls due, causing the payment to be overlooked, or might be temporarily low in cash. Most companies allow a grace period of 31 days after the date the premium is due. If you pay during this time, the insurance continues in force.

Five Points to Remember Before You Buy Hospital or Health Insurance

Here are five recommendations to help you get the most from your health insurance policy. The suggestions are based upon information from the American Medical Association, Association of Better Business Bureaus, the Institute of Life Insurance, and family finance counselors at numerous universities.

• *Deal with a reputable insurance agent or firm.* If you buy insurance through an agent, you will depend to a large extent upon his recommendations. So make sure that he is thoroughly trustworthy and reliable. He should be known by your bank, neighbors, or other businessmen in the community as a reputable representative who will have your best interests at heart.

If you deal with a company direct, make certain that it has passed the requirements set up by your state's insurance department and is licensed to operate there. Before dealing with a firm that does all its business by mail, make sure that your local Better Business Bureau has no record of complaints made against the firm by dissatisfied customers.

If you buy group insurance—the kind available only to employees in your firm or members of an organization to which you belong—you can generally rely upon the issuing company. If you have any doubts, consult the individual who was responsible for selecting it. Make sure that he has investigated it thoroughly and can vouch for its reliability.

• *Make certain of what you are getting.* Decide which features are most important to you. Suppose you want an income if you are laid up by illness or disability for longer than two or three months. Insurance protection until then may be less important, since your employer will pay your wages for a time. You will choose a policy that gives long-term benefits but has a waiting period in the beginning of the illness. After you have decided which features are best for your particular circumstances, compare policies on that basis.

You should know what specific benefits you are entitled to —and what benefits you will not get. It will pay to read the whole policy carefully, and to understand what all the words mean. If you still have questions, ask your insurance agent or a representative of the insurance company. Do not sign a contract until his answers satisfy you.

• *Protect your long-term rights.* As noted above, some companies reserve the right to cancel your policy if you do not seem to be a profitable customer. By refusing to renew, they deny you an extremely important privilege, and sharply reduce the value of your insurance. Your policies should continue in force as long as you—and not someone else—wants them to.

• *Make sure you can pay the premiums regularly.* Many young couples do not realize that when they commit themselves to insurance, they will have to pay regular premiums for years. Some buy expensive policies but find it difficult to keep them up in the slightest financial crisis. Under such circumstances, they cancel the policies, and are much worse off than if they had taken realistic, less expensive insurance at the beginning.

• *Review all your policies once a year.* If you have an agent, discuss with him whether policies taken out under different family conditions suit your needs today. Keep all your policies together and in a safe place—in a fire-resistant box at home or a safe deposit box. Both husband and wife, and adult children, should know where they are kept. They may be needed when you file a claim.

Your Answer to Sky-Rocketing Medical Bills?

Sky-rocketing medical costs, the steadily-rising fees of doctors who run their own business, and the fact that modern medicine has become too involved for any one doctor, have placed adequate medical care beyond the reach of millions of Americans with average incomes. More and more persons who cannot afford fees of up to $25 for an office visit to an ordinary doctor are joining "group practice" plans which guarantee a wide range of medical services for a specified fee each month. At present, most of these plans are open to groups of ten or more who work for the same employer and join at the same time.

I asked spokesmen for the Group Health Association to describe how such prepayment plans operate. Here is what they said:

A group of doctors, each with special training and experience, work together with trained technicians in well-equipped medical centers. One specialist in the group performs surgery, another delivers babies, another diagnoses obscure ailments in his special area, a fourth sets bones. Others are experts in the increasingly specialized phases of medicine, and each gives only the kind of service for which he has been professionally qualified.

In a medical group the doctors pool their knowledge, experience, and the plan's equipment. Result: Substantially lower costs for doctor services, x-rays, and other diagnostic tests. Few doctors in their own offices can afford the facilities which are available to doctors in group practice.

In one highly popular plan—the Group Health Association of Washington, D. C.—a family can be enrolled under a "premium" contract which provides complete medical and hospital care with few exceptions for $24.20 per month. For this fee, you get complete medical care in your GHA doctor's office, in the hospital and at home.

You pay only $5.00 for the first home call in any one illness —and no more. There is never a charge for an office visit whether for a routine check-up, treatment for injury or sickness, eye examinations, or emergency treatment. Laboratory exams, physical therapy treatments, x-rays and most other diagnostic tests are provided at no cost under this plan.

GHA patients receive complete obstetrical service at no extra cost, including pre-natal, delivery, and post-partum care. The member pays only the first $50 of the hospital bill for maternity care and also gets unlimited surgical care when it is needed.

Semi-private accommodations in any general hospital in the service area for an unlimited number of days per year also are provided. GHA will pay your entire general hospital bill without deduction.

Advocates of group practice medicine say that the medical care provided in this way is greatly superior to that which an individual doctor can provide in his office. "Every doctor in the group gets to know what his associates are doing," says the Group Health Association. "The day-to-day exchange of views and experience represents for each physician a continuing education and stimulus and the group as a whole is enabled to keep abreast of all the major developments of modern medicine.

"These additional benefits are possible because the medical group works as a team and pools its knowledge and resources. Enrollees select one of the family doctors on the staff as their doctor, and use other staff doctors as well.

"This group practice of medicine helps to detect and cure a member's illness before it develops into a serious problem. You are encouraged to have regular physical check-ups and to seek early treatment of any ailment. As a result you can get much better care than you probably would get otherwise."

GROUP DENTAL CARE: It is also possible to obtain dental insurance in a few places, where for a specific monthly fee most dental services will be provided. For instance, the Group Health Association of Washington also has a prepaid program which provides almost all types of dental treatment.

Before you can join the prepaid part of the plan, your teeth must be in good condition. You must pay the association to do all this work on a fee-for-service basis. Your regular prepaid service will start on the first day of the month after all of this dental care is completed.

You can then get the following services at no extra charge: Cleaning of teeth semi-annually or as needed; x-rays and examinations at regular intervals; sodium fluoride at the proper age; emergency care for relief of pain, fillings, root canal therapy and any necessary minor surgery (extraction of teeth, etc.).

The Washington group provides dentures, fixed bridgework,

jackets and inlays, and gum treatments for a 50 percent reduction of regular prices. Monthly membership costs in the prepaid group are $3.00 for each adult, $2.50 each for the first two children under 15 years in the family, and $2.25 for each additional child under 15 years.

chapter seven

HOW TO
USE A CHECKING ACCOUNT

You can save time and money by learning the proper ways to write and handle checks

Not many years ago, a typical husband or his wife set aside one day a month to paying bills. He or she trudged from store to store and from light company to phone company, paying their monthly debts in cash. Roughly, half the families in America still do this, despite the fact that it is costly in time and money.

The more efficient way is to open a checking account at your local bank. Then you can pay all your bills at your desk, writing checks and letting the mailman do the work. You will accomplish in 30 minutes what would otherwise take a day. Your money will be safe because you will not have to carry large amounts with you. You will have automatic receipts because your checks are returned to you after the bank pays off on them. And you will be better able to keep your accounts straight: You will receive a bank statement each month and will know exactly where you stand.

Here is what you should know about checking accounts. It is based upon material I obtained from officials of the American Bankers Association:

To open an account, just go to a commercial bank and ask to see the person in charge of new accounts. He will ask your name, address, telephone number and occupation, and perhaps ask for a reference or two. He will request that you sign a card exactly as you would sign your name in writing checks. In this way the bank can then be sure a check is authentic when it is presented for payment.

You will be given a supply of checks and possibly a passbook, in which your deposits will be listed. If the bank does not use passbooks, it will give a receipt each time you make a deposit.

If husband and wife open a joint account, either can make deposits or write checks. You can open such an account with "rights of survivorship"; if one person dies, the account automatically becomes the survivor's.

But joint accounts can sometimes present problems. You should always check deposits and withdrawals with each other so that both will know exactly what balance you have in the account and avoid writing a check for more than the balance. If that happens, your bank will probably send the check back marked "insufficient funds," and you will be embarrassed.

In most banks, you can open either a regular or a special checking account. In a regular account, you are expected to keep a minimum balance on deposit, generally $300 to $500. If your funds in a regular account drop below a minimum amount or you draw an excessive number of checks, you may have to pay a service charge to cover the bank's handling costs.

In a special account, no minimum balance is required. You need only enough money to cover any check you write. Usually you are asked to buy a book of checks when you open your account. When these are used up, you will have to buy more checks. These generally cost from 5 cents to 15 cents each. This may be the only charge the bank makes, but in some cases a maintenance charge of 25 to 50 cents per month is made.

In making a deposit in either account, you just write out

a deposit slip on which you record your name, address, date, and the amount being deposited. You are expected to list paper money and coins separately, and also to list each check being deposited.

How to Use Your Checkbook

It has two parts—stubs and checks. Whenever you make a deposit, add the amount to the previous balance carried on the stub. The stub thus serves to tell you how much you have in the bank at any given time. Before you write a check, fill out the stub with the check number, date, amount of the check, name of the person (or company) to whom it will be given, and the purpose of the payment. Your stubs can serve as a complete record of all the checks you draw.

After you complete the stub, write six different items in ink on the check itself.

1. Write the same day's date, except if it is a Sunday or holiday. Then date it the previous business day. If you write a future date, the bank will not honor your check until that time.

2. Write the check number. You should number your checks in order, so that you can keep track of them better.

3. After the printed words "Pay to the order of . . ." write the name of the person (or company) you want to pay. If you want to draw cash, write your check to the order of yourself, to "cash" or to "bearer." Everyone who wishes to cash your check—even yourself—must first endorse it by writing his signature on its back.

4. Write, in words, the amount to be paid. If you start writing as far to the left as possible, no one will be able to insert a word before it and raise the amount. Write pennies as a fraction of a hundred. Thus $2.86 will be written as "Two and $86/100$ Dollars." After you have written in the amount, fill in any unused space with a line.

5. Write the amount in figures. According to law, the amount in words is considered correct if it does not agree with the amount in figures. But many banks refuse checks when a difference exists. So make sure that words and figures agree.

6. Sign your name on the line at the bottom of the check. Your signature must resemble the one on the card you filled out when you opened your account. Since your signature makes the check valid, you should never sign blank checks and leave them around. Anyone could fill in the blanks, making a large sum payable to himself, and your bank would probably cash it because the signature is legitimate.

If you cross out, erase or change any part of the check, the bank will not accept it. If you make an error, tear up the check, and write a new one.

How Checks are Processed

When you write a check payable to another depositor of your bank, he simply endorses it and places it in his account. The bank deducts the amount from your balance and adds it to his.

When the recipient of your check uses a different bank, a special "clearing" arrangement is used. His bank will present this check to your bank for payment, and your bank will deduct the amount from your account. If your check is deposited out of town, several days may elapse before it clears. A bank official will be able to tell you how long a time will be required for the collection process to be completed.

As a matter of convenience, your bank will give you provisional credit as soon as you deposit a check. However, you are not free to draw cash against your deposit until your bank collects from the bank against which the check is drawn. If that bank refuses to pay, the amount will be deducted from your account and you will be notified. If you draw a check against funds which have not yet been collected, your bank may refuse to honor it.

Even after writing a check and giving it to someone, you can "stop payment." Simply ask your bank not to pay it if you wish. There is an extra charge for this service, but it may be worth it. Suppose you order something from a store and pay by check. It is delivered in poor condition. You call the store and get no satisfaction. You fear that you may be stuck for the merchandise if the store cashes your check. You need only ask your bank to withhold payment. You can do this by a written order, by telegram, telephone, or by filling out a stop-payment request form. Of course, your notice must reach the bank before the check is paid.

You may be asked to pay by certified check when you buy a house or a car or engage in other dealings. This is one on which a bank stamps the word "certified" along with its name and the signature of an officer. By this act it guarantees to pay the check when it is presented. Of course, it first makes sure that you have sufficient funds on deposit, and it sets them aside for this purpose.

In certifying a check, the bank in effect promises to pay it when properly endorsed. For this reason, if you lose one, your bank may require a bond for twice its amount before crediting your account or certifying a replacement.

Never destroy a certified check. If you have one which will not be used, return it to the bank and deposit it for credit to your account.

A "Bank Money Order" or "Cashier's Check" is the bank's own check. It guarantees to pay the stated amount out of its own funds. You can buy a bank money order or a cashier's check by paying the amount of it plus a service charge. When properly endorsed it may be cashed, or it may be deposited in any bank.

What You Should Know About Endorsements

Before you can cash or deposit a check made out to you, you must endorse it by signing it on the back at the left end.

If a check has been made out to you and you wish to give it to another, you must first endorse it. The other person must also endorse it before he can cash it.

If your name is misspelled or incomplete, write your first endorsement in the same way. Below it write your correct signature.

Never endorse a check until you get to the bank. Your personal endorsement makes the check negotiable; if it is lost with your endorsement on it, the finder may cash it.

You can use a restrictive endorsement in making deposits. If you write "for deposit only" over your signature, it can be placed in your account only.

You can also use a special endorsement to pass title to a check. Suppose you owe $50 to John Doe and receive a $50 check. On the back, write "Pay to the order of John Doe," and sign your name. He can either cash it or endorse it over to someone else. However, your bank will probably frown on too many endorsements.

Balancing Your Checkbook

Every month or so, your bank will send you a statement showing your deposits and withdrawals during that period and your balance at the beginning and end of the period. You will also receive checks signed by you which the bank has cashed during that time.

Here is how to balance your own records with your bank's statement:

1. Sort your checks numerically or by the date issued.
2. Reduce your checkbook balance by the amount of any

How to Use a Checking Account   119

service charges for the period which you have not previously deducted.

3. Enter statement balance—$ . . .

4. On your stubs, check off each check which has been paid by the bank. List all checks you have issued but which the bank has not paid. Subtract the total of these unpaid checks here. . . . $ . . .
$\overline{\$ \ldots}$

5. Add any deposit you made later than the date of the statement. $ . . .

6. Your checkbook balance should be the same as your total now. If not, repeat your arithmetic carefully. If it appears that the bank has erred, you should report the error at once.

In any event, carefully file the statement, cancelled checks, and stubs in a safe place. If a dispute over a bill arises later, your cancelled check can prove that you made the payment. Cancelled checks will also help you prove claims of income tax deductions for charity, etc.

Ten Don'ts to Remember

Don't write a check in pencil.

Don't make a check out to "Cash" until you get to the bank where you can cash it yourself.

Don't endorse a check until you are at the bank to cash or deposit it.

Don't wait to cash checks—deposit them. A bank may not accept a check which is several months old.

Don't fail to record each check you write in the stub of your checkbook.

Don't neglect to number each check.

If you have a joint account, don't forget to keep a combined, complete record of all checks drawn by *both* parties, so that your balance will be correct.

Don't write a large check without first making sure you have sufficient funds in the bank to cover it.

Don't leave your old cancelled checks where they may be lost or stolen. They are your receipts for payments. If a forger obtained one, he might use it to copy your signature.

If any numbered blank checks are stolen, don't wait to "see if they turn up." Notify your bank immediately.

chapter eight

A SHORT COURSE ON STOCKS AND BONDS

Clear-cut advice which can increase your chances of making money when you invest

In creating your financial program, most experts agree, you should take the following steps:

First make sure that you can cover your living expenses—your outlays for food, clothing, shelter and other necessities—without going into debt.

Then make sure that your family will be provided for by insurance if the breadwinner dies.

Then build a savings account with at least half a year's income to pay for unexpected medical or hospital bills and to see you through other possible financial rough spots.

Not until you have adequate liquid savings—money you can get at once if you have to—should you consider investing in stocks and bonds. For while these may bring you a profit, they also involve possible loss.

What Investing Really Means

We live in a capitalist economy. It takes money to run our public utilities, factories, stores, banks, insurance companies and other enterprises which provide the necessities and luxuries of our daily lives. That money comes from individuals—men of great wealth, professional men, shopkeepers, civil service employees, farmers, factory workers, widows—in short, everybody. Surveys have shown that 12,500,000 individuals in this country have invested their capital in one or more business operations. Some 110,000,000 are indirect owners of businesses through their insurance policies, pension funds, union dues and savings which have been invested in various corporations. So even if you do not own stocks or bonds directly, you probably own some indirectly through these other mediums.

An investor puts up the money to operate a business. If it prospers, he may share in the profits and his investment may increase in value. If it fails, the corporation's value declines and his proportionate share is less.

When you buy a share of common stock, you become a part-owner of the business and can help decide how it should be operated. With your fellow stockholders, you can hire and fire its actual managers. You are like a citizen who can decide how his country should be run. However, the number of a stockholder's votes is directly proportionate to the number of shares he owns.

Buying stock is like buying a house, car or other property. You can examine the property, decide what it is worth to you, then offer that price to someone who wishes to sell. If your offer matches what he will accept, a transaction is made. If a difference exists, you must raise your offering price or the seller must lower his asking price, or there is no sale. Hundreds of thousands of shares are usually outstanding in each of the companies listed on the New York Stock Exchange and other exchanges throughout the United States and Canada. These shares may change hands frequently. By consulting the stock market tables in your daily newspaper, you can tell what they can be bought or sold for at any time.

You can invest your capital in business enterprises in several ways. For example:

• *You can buy common stock in a corporation.* These make

you a part-owner. You profit or lose as the company profits or loses. You have no guarantee that you will be paid regular dividends or that the stock will be worth more when you sell it.

• *You can buy preferred stock.* This entitles you to receive dividends at a fixed rate—perhaps $5.00 a year, perhaps payable at the rate of $1.25 every three months. Buying ordinary preferred stock is like lending money to the company. If it prospers, you get the designated dividends—but generally no more than that. If it loses money, you will generally get dividends. However, the company has the right to "pass" them. In most cases, you'll get the "passed" dividends when it again makes money.

• *You can buy bonds.* These also have a fixed rate of interest. When you buy bonds, you lend money to the corporation. You are a debtor, not a part owner, and do not share in profits or losses. If it does not pay interest on its bonds at the times stipulated, you and the other bondholders may have the right to sell its property to get what is owed to you.

• *You can buy convertible preferred stock or convertible debentures (a form of bond).* You will receive dividend or interest payments regularly, and you will also have the right to convert your stock into common shares under specified conditions. Suppose you buy a share of ABC convertible preferred with a basic value of $100. The "convertible" feature allows you to exchange it for five common shares whenever you choose. Obviously, you would retain it if the common shares sold for less than $20. But if they jumped to $30, your preferred would be worth $150. Once you convert preferred shares to common, however, you lose the assurance of regular dividends.

• *You can buy "participating preferred."* These shares have a fixed rate of interest, but if the corporation declares a certain dividend on the common stocks, you may be entitled to extra dividends as well.

• *You can buy "warrants" or "rights."* These give you the option of buying common stock at certain prices. Example: A company issues warrants entitling holders to buy its stock at $6.75 until 1970. The stock now sells for $8.00. Thus the warrants are worth at least $1.25—the difference between what they entitle you to buy the stock for and what it is worth. If the stock sells for less than $6.75, the warrants will be worth only what speculators might pay for the chance that it might rise and make them valuable.

What Investment Is Best for You?

Before you invest a penny, you should know what you hope to gain. To be reasonable, this hope should be based upon your age and savings, whether you own your home and have enough life insurance, and also your temperament—your ability to take risks without worry. All these factors are important, because no one investment is ideal for everybody. The choice you make will depend on your own personal needs. Most people have one of three basic motives when they invest:

Many want to be reasonably sure of getting a dependable return on their money even in a depression. These people may be attracted by the bonds of solid corporations. Risks here are at a minimum—but interest rates are relatively low, too.

Other investors want better interest or dividend rates plus a chance to sell out at a higher price if the company prospers. They must take a corresponding risk that dividends and the value of their investment will be lower if the company does poorly. The degree of risk depends upon the company, the industry it represents and the condition of the economy generally. For instance, a major public utility might endure a depression better than a manufacturer of luxuries the public could do without. But there probably would be less chance that the price of the utility's stock would increase sharply.

Other investors care little about current dividends. They

have heard of automobile firms started with thousands of dollars that were soon worth millions, and they want to make their fortune the same way. Of course, dozens of new companies fail to achieve any substantial growth for each one that mushrooms. So the risk in finding a spectacular stock is great. It corresponds to the potential profit—*if* you choose the right company.

Here are four case histories showing why you must consider your own background and financial history in order to make sound investment decisions.

Ann Brown is 56, a widow and childless. Her husband just died and left a total estate of $80,000. She has now held a job for 33 years, but can no longer do a full day's work. She must depend upon that estate to produce income all her life and obviously cannot afford risks. An investment adviser might recommend a common stock in a solid company which has paid dividends in good and bad times, or preferred stock or bonds which will keep her capital intact while giving her a steady income.

Dick and Mary Sealy are middle-aged and have three grown children. Their $20,000 home is all paid for. They have $8,000 on deposit with their local Savings and Loan Association to cushion them if "a rainy day" comes along. They also have about $5,000 which they want to invest. He would like to retire in about ten years. They can afford some risks, but should not stake their $5,000 on a company which may prove a failure. Their best bet? A broker might suggest common stock in an industry which seems to have a secure future and some prospects of growing.

Bill Klein is 26 and his wife Barbara is 23. They have one son, a home, and Bill has a good job with fine prospects for advancement. They have inherited $3,000 and hope to make it grow into a good-sized fund for their son's college education. Since they can afford more risk than the widow or older couple, an investment counsellor might suggest shares in a company which may not pay dividends now but has great prospects for the future.

Arthur Pembroke is a corporation executive who earns $80,000 a year. He has $20,000 to invest. He does not want a dividend-paying stock because he is in a high tax bracket and would have little of the dividends left after the tax collector's cut. He prefers a stock which might greatly increase in price. He could sell it after six months and pay no more than 25 percent of his profit in taxes. Thus the opportunity to obtain these lower tax rates might influence where and how you should invest.

How to Decide Where to Invest

It is always a good principle to get the best professional advice you can before you spend your money. Select a broker with care, perhaps choosing him on the recommendation of your banker, lawyer or other individual whose financial judgment you respect. Your broker should be a member of a recognized exchange such as the New York Stock Exchange and American Stock Exchange, or of the National Association of Security Dealers. You can ask him to help select stocks or bonds for you, or he can provide the information you will need to make your own intelligent choice.

Stock brokers have masses of information—official company reports, statements of company officials, independent studies, etc.—upon which to base a judgment. They have manuals such as *Moody's* and *Standard and Poor's*, which contain detailed reports on all major companies—their history, financial standing, past earnings and dividends records. From these manuals, you can learn how much a company is worth, how much capital it has to work with, how large an inventory it carries, how much money it owes and is owed, the estimated value of its plant and equipment. Thus you can get a clear picture of its operations.

You can learn much about day-to-day changes in company fortunes—new orders, acquisitions or mergers, seasonal sales reports, changes in top management, etc.—by reading a daily newspaper which features financial news. Many experienced investors find the daily *Wall Street Journal* a must. They often read one or more of the magazines which report on company and industry trends—such publications as *Barron's, Business Week, Financial World, Forbes,* the *Magazine of Wall Street.*

Whether you obtain the information yourself or a broker does it for you, you should have up-to-date data about any company in which you invest. You should have answers to these questions:

• *What does the company do?* Some businesses probably have seen their peaks. An ice manufacturer might not have a glittering future in this era when automatic refrigerators are everywhere. Other industries may foresee new and highly-profitable markets. Example: the drug manufacturing industry after World War II, when dozens of wonder medicines were developed. But before you buy shares in a company with promising prospects, be sure that other alert investors have not already bid prices so high that even if the promise is fulfilled, the stock may not be worth the asking price.

• *What are its annual earnings?* You can get this information by consulting recent annual and quarterly reports. Moody's and Standard and Poor's manuals list company earnings for recent years. Thus you can determine whether a firm has consistent profits or makes money one year and loses it the next. Investors searching for growth situations favor concerns which consistently earn more money year after year. On the other hand, a corporation may be in a declining stage if its annual earnings go down steadily.

Investment experts often appraise stocks on the basis of price-earnings ratios—how many times the price is greater than the company's profits after taxes. For instance, before the great bull market of the 1950s got under way, some stocks sold for

5 times their annual earnings and investment advisers recommended them as bargains. Ten years later, the same issues sold for 30 times earnings and were believed to be over-priced.

When compared to the total dollar-volume of sales, a company's earnings tell you how efficient it is in making a profit. It may make only a few cents on every dollar of sales while its competitor earns double the amount. Analysts might conclude that the second company is managed better and therefore is a more desirable investment.

• *What is its dividend-paying record?* Does it distribute most of its profits to its stockholders or retain them to finance future operations? Investors who desire current income favor the liberal dividend-payer; those who seek growth potential prefer the other type.

• *What is its debt?* If it has many debts outstanding, common stockholders could benefit, for they will get all the profits and the debtors will get only a fixed rate of interest. But if the company loses money, it must still pay interest charges on the debt. In this case, the common stockholders will suffer. You may wish to consider whether a company with proportionately large amounts of bonds, preferred stocks and bank loans outstanding will be able to pay dividends to common stockholders as consistently as another company without large fixed charges.

• *What is its "book value"?* In other words, how much would it be worth if it sold all its assets, paid all its debts and went out of business? Investment analysts today do not consider the answer as important as they once did, but "book value" sometimes tells an intriguing story.

Suppose a company's assets are worth $50 per share after all its debts are paid, and its stock sells for only $10. There may be a strong chance that it might close up or merge with a more prosperous concern. In either case, the stock would probably be worth more or a change in management or company policy might make its assets work more effectively. Earnings might rise sharply and raise the price of the stock.

On the other hand, a company whose shares have a book value of $10 but sell for $50 probably makes a large profit on a small capital investment. Competitors might move in to make similar large profits.

- *Will some new development seriously affect the company's future?* In late 1958, alert investors might have foreseen that the Castro government in Cuba was moving leftward and might seize the holdings of American corporations there. If you failed to investigate these possibilities and bought shares of an American sugar company for $50, your stock would soon sell for $14. Many motion picture companies keep negatives to all their old films, but value them at only $1 on their books. An analyst might have foreseen that these films could be sold to television for millions, making the companies worth much more than was apparent on the surface.

Answers to the above and similar questions are considered by experienced security analysts before they recommend a particular stock. Even then, of course, the recommendation will depend upon the investor's individual circumstances and objectives.

How the Stock Market Works

Contrary to a common belief, a stock exchange does not buy or sell securities. Rather, it provides the meeting place where representatives of people with stock to sell can meet representatives of those who want to buy.

An exchange itself has nothing to do with prices. These are determined by buyers and sellers through their brokers. But the exchange has extensive rules to make sure that companies whose shares are traded on its floor regularly provide investors with all the information needed to decide intelligently whether to buy or sell. It also prescribes the conduct of members in dealing with the public. The purpose is to prevent crooked business and to protect stock buyers and sellers all over the country.

Let us follow a typical transaction on the New York Stock Exchange to see exactly what happens when you buy or sell the shares of a company traded there.

Suppose you live in a city thousands of miles from New York where there is a branch office for a brokerage firm belonging to the exchange. You first visit the broker's office and announce that you would like to open an account.

A registered representative gives you an application form to fill out. The only information required is your name, address, age, occupation, name and address of employment, and a reference or two.

From now on, you can personally visit the office when you wish to buy or sell, or you need merely place your order by phone. Some individuals buy and sell stock almost every week, yet never see a broker. All their transactions are quickly handled by phone.

If you wish, you can place an order without consulting anyone, or you can ask your broker to suggest suitable investments. Obviously he will be better able to help you if he understands your financial position, what objectives you hope to achieve by buying stocks or bonds, and what risks you are prepared to take. Otherwise he cannot advise your properly.

Most brokerage firms maintain research departments, staffed with analysts who devote their time to studies of various corporations, industries and the economy at large. They try to obtain as much information as possible upon which to base a sound investment decision. They constantly issue up-to-date reports which you can obtain without obligation. In fact, brokerage houses will make so much information available to you that there is no excuse for buying into a company about which you know little or nothing.

Let us say that you have investigated thoroughly and have decided to buy shares of the ABC Company. The stock sells at

A Short Course on Stocks and Bonds

about $43 a share. Thus 100 shares will cost about $4,300, plus a commission to be paid your broker. This commission will amount to about $36.50. It is never larger than 6 percent of the total price, and that is on a $100 transaction. On a purchase or sale involving $600, it would be less than 2 percent—$11. On a $3,000 transaction, it is only one percent, and on a $10,000 trade, it is less than ½ of 1 percent. These commissions are minimum charges established by the Stock Exchange.

It is between 10 A.M. and 3:30 P.M. Eastern Standard Time—the hours the Exchange is open. Your broker wires New York for the exact price. He learns that shares are offered at $43 and that others on the floor are willing to pay $42.50. With certain exceptions, all transactions on the Exchange floor involve 100-share units or "round lots." (You can buy an "odd lot"—less than 100 shares—by paying 12½ or 25 cents extra per share, depending upon the price).

Your broker assures you that you can now buy ABC at no more than $43. Let us say that you authorize him to buy 100 shares at the market, meaning at the best possible price. You can also set an exact price—say 42¾—beyond which you will not go. But it might be impossible to execute your order, since the stock might not be available at that price. When you place orders at the market, you give your broker room in which to negotiate.

Your home-town broker wires your instructions to New York. Within minutes your order is placed in the hands of the broker's representative on the Exchange floor. He walks quickly to a post where ABC stock is always traded and a specialist who maintains contacts between buyers and sellers quotes the highest bid and lowest offering prices.

On a very active day during which 4,000,000 shares are sold, the situation might change greatly within a few minutes. A stock might sell for $1 more one minute than the next. This fluctuation is another reason why brokers often recommend buying at the market. Then you can buy or sell regardless of market conditions. In this case, however, the situation has not changed since the order was placed.

Your floor representative knows that a bid of 42½ ($42.50) will not be accepted, but that a bid of 43 will be. He offers 42¾ ($42.75). Another broker with stock to sell accepts the proposition, since it is a better offer than any others that have been made. If necessary, your broker would have gone to 43.

Each broker notes on a pad who bought or sold the stock, and the price paid. These are records for the bookkeeping departments of the brokerage houses involved. The specialist also notes the price, and it is reported to the stock exchange ticker department. All over the country, customers in brokerage offices can see on the tape that 100 shares of ABC have just been sold for $42.75. Within a few minutes, your representative receives a report on the trade and relays the news to you.

You will receive formal confirmation by mail, and you must pay for the stock within four days. The person selling the stock also is expected to deliver it within four days. His broker then turns his signed certificate of transfer over to your broker for the purchase price. Your broker will then send it to a transfer agent who will issue a new certificate for 100 shares in your name.

Experienced traders use different types of orders to dictate exactly how much they pay for a stock. Suppose you think ABC shares might soon drop to $40. Your broker will take your order, "good until cancelled," to buy them at that price, and will enter it with the floor specialist. If the price reaches $40, they will be sold to you or to persons who have placed a similar order before you did. You can sell stock the same way. Suppose that after you buy it, the price rises to $48 and you doubt that it will go higher. You can give your broker an order, also "good until cancelled," to sell as soon as $48 is offered.

Another variation is a stop-loss order. Suppose you do not want to hold the shares if the price falls below $35. You can leave an order to sell at that point. If someone else sells at $35,

A Short Course on Stocks and Bonds

your shares will be sold to the next buyer who comes along.

Stop-loss orders are handy devices for the experienced, but dangerous for a novice. Before using one, you would do well to discuss with your broker exactly what you hope to achieve by this step. He may suggest another action better suited to your purposes.

Buying and Selling "Over the Counter"

The New York Stock Exchange is the most widely known institution of its kind, where the shares of most of America's greatest corporations are traded. The shares of thousands of companies are also bought and sold at the American Stock Exchange and regional exchanges throughout the country. But the greatest number of corporate securities are sold in the over the counter market. Here is where you might buy or sell shares of your local department store, factory, bank, and medium-sized companies located all over the country.

Actually there is no special market place for trading over the counter. Rather, there is a network of almost 2,000 individual dealers throughout the country who will buy and sell stock for individual corporations.

Suppose you wish to buy shares in the MNM insurance company. Instead of wiring to New York for the latest price, your broker consults a "quotation service sheet," published daily, listing the highest known price buyers will pay for a specific stock and the lowest price sellers will take. He will negotiate with the prospective sellers and strive to buy the stock at the lowest available price, plus commission.

Shares of many excellent corporations are bought and sold over the counter. However, most newspapers do not carry daily quotations and it may be difficult for you to learn the latest prices. Shares traded over the counter are paid for, delivered, and transferred the same as those bought and sold on an exchange.

Mutual Funds and What They Do

In effect, mutual funds offer you the opportunity to buy the securities of dozens or hundreds of corporations by buying the shares of one company which has invested in all the others. Thus your eggs can go into many baskets.

"A mutual fund or open-end investment company," according to George A. Mooney, executive director of the National Association of Investment Companies, "is a company which combines the investment funds of many people whose investment goals are similar, and in turn invests those funds in a wide variety of securities. Closed-end companies perform much the same service for their shareholders.

"In addition to spreading risk by diversification, investment companies employ professional investment men to select and continuously supervise the investments of the investment companies, which means those of the shareholders.

"Thus, investment companies seek to do for the individual investor what he might do for himself if he had the time, the inclination, the background and experience and sufficient money to spread his investment among many different businesses.

"As individual companies, the members of the National Association of Investment Companies have a wide range of investment objectives, management policies and degrees of risk and profit opportunities.

"Some companies aim for long-term growth of capital and income. Others stress current income. Still others put capital stability as their first goal. Some investment companies concentrate almost entirely on the so-called blue-chip common stocks issued by large and well-known corporations which are leaders in their respective fields. Others may specialize in so-called growth company stocks, which because of the nature of their products or services or financing or other reasons are believed to offer opportunities for substantially increased income and value in the future.

"Some companies invest in varying proportions of fixed-income securities and common stocks. A few invest only in preferred stocks and some few others invest only in bonds. The largest number by far, however, emphasize diversified investment in common stocks.

"Since prices of all securities may go either up or down, the investment company can not promise to return a certain number of dollars or pay any specific amount of income.

"Investment companies are the only financial institutions through which investors of moderate means can share directly in the risks and rewards of equity investment under professional management, conservatively, and with the protection of broad diversification and continued supervision.

"Basically there is no difference in the way the open-end and closed-end investment companies carry on their business. The significant distinction between them lies in the way in which their shares are bought and sold. All mutual funds stand ready at any time to redeem outstanding shares—generally at asset value—when presented by the investor. In addition, most mutual funds continuously offer new shares to investors at a public offering price based on current net asset value.

"A closed-end company, on the other hand, generally has a fixed capitalization with a fixed number of shares outstanding. Shares of some closed-end companies are traded on the New York Stock Exchange or other exchanges, while shares of others are available in the over-the-counter market. These shares may sell for more or less than the actual value of the assets they represent. It all depends on how the buying public feels about them."

Do mutual funds really perform as well as they promise and do mutual fund stockholders get their money's worth? *Forbes* Magazine of Business compares the performances of the different funds each year. Its 1960 appraisal stated:

"To a degree, the answer is yes. Certainly the funds have done a creditable job keeping up with the averages." While the average price of 500 representative common stocks climbed 143.77% over the entire six-and-three-quarter year bull market, Forbes reported that its average of common stock mutual funds rose a remarkably similar 140.64%.

The commission you must pay when you buy mutual shares is generally about 8%. Thus if you have $1,000 to invest, only $920 is used for the mutual fund shares, and $80 goes to the salesman, brokerage firms, etc. Even if the value of the shares increases, you may have to wait a year or longer before your shares are worth what you paid. However, for investors of moderate means who seek diversification, this sales charge is not considerably higher than the effective cost of buying stock directly on a stock exchange. In transactions of a few shares made by small investors, the commissions involved in buying on an exchange might even be higher. As an example, to purchase one share of each of the 30 stocks in the Dow Jones Industrial Average would cost about $2,700 and involve a commission of some 5½%. If these were sold at about the same price level, another 5½% charge would be deducted for a total of about 11%. Mutual funds generally make no charge on redemption.

Another important point is that you should look upon mutual funds as long term investments. They are not designed to be used in the same manner as individual stock issues to be purchased and sold on short or intermediate considerations. As complete investment services, they are intended to serve long range goals.

In advising people on more effective use of their money, experts generally find it important to stress the steps that one should take selecting an investment. In the case of investment companies, it is generally agreed that the most important thing is that a person select a company with investment objectives which are the same as his own. He should decide what his long term requirements are and the degree of risk he can afford and is willing to take to fulfill them. He must then select a company with similar objectives which seems in a good position to carry them out. In this area, the services of a trained investment dealer or broker are of utmost importance.

If you take the trouble to investigate, you can find mutual funds which sell shares directly to the public with little or no commission involved. Some of these companies have achieved better results than some which can be bought only by paying a commission. And some commission-less or "no-load" mutual funds have poorer records.

Forbes Magazine, published at 70 Fifth Ave., New York 11, N.Y., issues a yearly box-score showing how the different funds have performed in the preceding few years. You may use this as a guide to help you decide what its performance may be in the future. You can obtain a list of all funds, with their addresses, from the National Association of Investment Companies, 61 Broadway, New York 6, New York. If a particular fund appeals to you, you can ask your broker about it or—if it is a "no-load fund"—you can write for its literature.

What You Should Know About Automatic Investing Plans

In order to attract the "little fellow" who might be unable to invest more than $40 in stocks every quarter, the New York Stock Exchange began its Monthly Investment Plan in 1954.

Under this plan, you agree to buy a certain stock every month or every quarter or so. You tell the broker how much you intend to invest regularly, and also choose one of the 1200 stocks listed in the Exchange in which to invest. (The broker will, of course, recommend certain stock for your particular purposes if asked to do so.)

The agreement is not binding. You can start it and stop it when you wish, even skip a few payments if you have to, and then resume your regular purchases again.

Each time you make a payment, the broker buys as many shares of stock as possible. Say you select a stock selling around $43 and plan to invest $100 in it each quarter. Your first payment will buy two shares of stock, plus the broker's commission, and leave something left over. The broker will apply this toward the purchase of a full share and credit your account with a fraction of a share.

The Monthly Investment Plan embodies a principle that has proved highly successful for some college endowment funds and individual investors. This is the principle of dollar-averaging: By using the same number of dollars to buy stock at regular intervals, you obtain more shares when the stock is low in price than when it is high. As a result, over a period of time, your average price per share will be on the low side. If the long-term trend of stock prices is upward, your average profit per share will be higher than if you had just bought a set number of shares each time.

Under the Monthly Investment Plan, dividends can be credited to your account and automatically used to buy more shares. This automatic re-investment of dividends enables you to increase your holdings more readily than you might by buying stock without benefit of it.

Most brokers would probably agree with this analysis:

Dollar-cost averaging will generally prove profitable with one exception—if the stock you select goes down and stays down. Your best profits are made if your stock has an early decline and then rises above the highest price you paid.

It takes a certain stubbornness to continue dollar-averaging as your stock declines. Moreover, you must be ready to lay out the necessary cash regardless of the price of the stock. And you must be prepared to leave your money invested when things look blackest. You will lose out if you must sell when your stock is priced lower than its average cost.

The same "monthly investment" principle is used to sell many mutual plans. In some cases, the buyer may be asked to

A Short Course on Stocks and Bonds 139

sign a contract requiring him to invest a certain number of dollars at regular specified intervals. If you buy a mutual funds plan this way, make sure that you will be able to continue it for several years, at least. Otherwise you may lose a great deal. Here is why: A large part of your first payment is used to cover the salesman's commission, and is deducted from the amount placed in your investment account. As a result of these deductions, if you disposed of your shares at the end of a year, you probably would have a severe loss.

Like the Monthly Investment Plan, mutual contractual plans give the advantage of "dollar-averaging" when employed over long periods. They are a special help to persons who cannot carry out systematic savings programs on their own initiative.

Ten Ways to Avoid Getting Gypped on Stocks and Bonds

Most brokers offer a true service to their clients by recommending securities in which they sincerely believe or by providing all the facts and figures an investor needs to make an intelligent decision of his own. But it is inevitable that gyps will find their way into an area in which billions of dollars change hands every year.

To avoid the danger of financial disaster at the hands of sharp-shooters and racketeers, here are ten rules you should follow before you buy *any* security. The rules were compiled by the Better Business Bureau of New York City in cooperation with the New York Stock Exchange, American Stock Exchange, Association of Stock Exchange Firms, National Association of Securities Dealers, Inc., and the Investment Bankers Association of America:

• *Don't buy on tips or rumors.* If you do, you almost surely will regret it. The inside dope on fabulous rewards to come is often imaginary. Get the facts.

• *Know your broker or dealer.* A stranger eager to let you in on something probably is not a responsible securities dealer. He may just be issuing a cordial invitation to pour your money down the drain—his drain. You can check with the Better Business Bureau or your bank.

• *Think before buying.* Few purchases of stocks or bonds are so important that they must be snapped up the minute you hear about them. Take time to consider, and chances are the bargain will still be available.

• *Beware of telephone pitches.* If a stranger from an unknown firm phones you to sell you a stock or bond you never heard of, he probably is calling a sucker list. He may offer pie-in-the-sky promises but all he wants is your money.

• *Guard against high-pressure sales.* The more insistent a salesman gets, the more cautious you should be. Remember: "If you buy on the basis of inside dope, the 'dope' could turn out to be you."

• *Beware of get-rich-quick promises.* Rumor mongers want you to think they want to make money for you. But just call on your common sense. If the deal is really such a bonanza, why is he sharing it with strangers?

• *Be sure you understand the risks.* An honest securities broker or dealer never guarantees a profit. Unlike the sharpshooter, he does not obscure the fact that prices can go down as well as up.

• *Get all the facts.* If you are solicited by telephone, tell the salesman to put all the information and advice in writing and mail it to you. Then save it for future reference. The law requires a company to publish the truth and nothing but the truth in its prospectus. So read everything completely and carefully.

• *When in doubt, find out.* If you don't understand all the written information, consult a person who does. "It's better to be embarrassed by lack of knowledge now, than lack of funds later."

• *Investigate before you invest.* Give at least as much consideration to buying securities as you would to buying a home, a car or other valuable property.

chapter nine

THERE IS AN ART
TO BUYING A HOUSE

Here are tests to tell you if you are the home-owning type—and what you can afford to pay

Most couples hope to have their own homes some day. A "place of your own" is part of the American dream. It connotes contented living, good surroundings for your children to grow up in, and security in your old age.

The Federal Government makes it attractive by letting you deduct local taxes from your income tax, as well as the interest you pay on your mortgage. Lending institutions also make it attractive with mortgages you can pay off month by month, like rent. As a result, when you buy a home you generally get more for the money you spend on housing—and you own it free and clear after twenty or twenty-five years, when your last mortgage payment has been made. Gradually paying off a mortgage therefore is one of the best possible ways of saving. Moreover, you pay a lower rate of interest on the money you borrow than on any other loan you can make.

Owning a home has many definite emotional advantages. It gives you a feeling of security—a sense of belonging to your community, which renters seldom or never achieve. It gives you freedom: You can improve your property without fearing that the landlord will force you to move next year or won't like what you have done. You can work around your house, making necessary repairs, knowing that you—and not someone else—will benefit from your efforts.

But home ownership is not for everyone. Even if you can easily afford to buy a house, you may not be the type. In fact, certain definite conditions should exist before you take on the pleasures—and problems—of home ownership. As vice president of the Washington Heights Federal Savings and Loan Association of New York, John H. Seiter checks on the records of thousands of home buyers a year. Most will make a success as home-owners, but some will not. To determine which category you belong in, he says, here are some questions you should ask yourself:

• *Are you reasonably secure in your job?* Obviously, you will be a nervous wreck if you take on long-term responsibilities when you lack the assurance that you will keep your position.

• *Are you likely to stay in the same town where you live now?* Some corporations often transfer their employees to different sections of the country for two- or three-year stretches, to give them experience in different phases of the firm's operations. If you may be transferred at any time, you probably should not own a home until your employment situation becomes more stable.

• *Can you take financial responsibilities without undue worry?* Some people exaggerate the burdens of owning a home. Realizing that they will have to make mortgage payments every month for twenty years, they worry that the mortgage might be foreclosed some time, that they might lose their savings if the neighborhood becomes run-down, and so on. If you are the type to lie awake nights wondering how you'll make the payments five years from now, you obviously won't enjoy your possessions as you should. You might be well advised to rent an apartment or a house you can move from when you choose and which you needn't worry about for longer than a month at a time.

• *Will you be happy living in one place for a long period—*

perhaps fifteen or more years? Some couples like to move about, trying this location one year, another location the next. But when such moves involve the buying and selling of houses, they become prohibitively expensive, since mortgage and legal fees and real estate agents' commissions must be paid. So they are out of the question for most people.

• *Are you willing to give your house your personal attention?* A renter can trot to the golf course on Saturday afternoon while the landlord or his plumber fixes the leaking pipe. As an owner, you'll have to make this and similar repairs yourself— or pay to have them done, and watch tradesmen growing rich off you. Most home owners spend several hours a week doing repair and maintenance jobs because the cost of having someone repair a leaky faucet or mow the lawn is more than they care to pay.

• *Do you get along well with neighbors?* If you rent an apartment in the city, you can come and go as you please— perhaps not even knowing the name of the occupant next door. When you buy a house, however, you are expected to be friendly and to join your neighbors in community projects.

If you can answer "yes" to most of these questions, you probably could make a good adjustment. Owning a home probably could give you its traditional satisfactions—a feeling of security, pride of possession, a sense of accomplishment.

What Can You Afford to Pay?

A few generations ago, most families waited until they had the full price before they considered buying a house. Many were ashamed to be in debt. Today, however, the usual thing is to buy a house with a small down payment, to borrow the rest from a savings and loan association or other lender, and to give a mortgage as security.

The type of mortgage generally used is known as "the regular amortized mortgage loan." The home-owner agrees to pay

WHERE U. S. HOME MORTGAGES ARE PLACED
(Based on Dollar Volume)

Year	Savings and Loan Associations	Savings Banks	Commercial Banks	Insurance Companies	All Other Lenders	Total
1940	31.8%	4.2%	25.0%	8.2%	30.7%	100.0%
1941	31.6	4.6	24.6	8.5	30.7	100.0
1942	29.7	4.2	22.5	9.2	34.5	100.0
1943	32.0	3.9	19.5	7.3	37.3	100.0
1944	33.9	3.6	19.1	5.6	37.8	100.0
1945	35.8	3.8	19.4	4.4	36.6	100.0
1946	32.9	5.2	25.6	4.8	31.5	100.0
1947	31.1	5.1	25.6	7.2	31.0	100.0
1948	30.5	6.3	22.4	8.6	32.2	100.0
1949	30.9	6.3	20.7	8.8	33.3	100.0
1950	31.3	6.6	20.8	10.0	31.3	100.0
1951	32.3	6.2	20.5	9.8	31.2	100.0
1952	35.8	6.3	20.0	7.9	30.0	100.0
1953	37.4	6.7	18.6	7.5	29.8	100.0
1954	36.2	6.5	18.5	7.7	31.1	100.0
1955	36.7	6.5	19.7	6.8	30.3	100.0
1956	35.2	6.7	20.2	6.6	31.3	100.0
1957	38.0	5.9	17.6	6.1	32.4	100.0
1958	38.4	6.0	19.0	5.3	31.3	100.0
1959	40.6	5.5	18.1	4.7	31.1	100.0

Source: Federal Home Loan Bank Board.

a fixed amount each month for the duration of the mortgage—generally twenty years. Some of his payment will reduce the debt owed on the mortgage. Another part of the monthly payment will cover interest on the money he has borrowed to purchase the house. Another part will cover taxes on the property, and still another may be applied toward insurance. This kind of mortgage has proved highly satisfactory for everyone. You increase your investment in the house by making regular payments like rent, the lending institution gets its interest regularly, taxes are paid on time, and insurance covers possible loss due to fire or other damage.

How much you will have to pay each month under a mortgage plan of this kind will depend upon these factors:

• *Amount of your down payment.* Obviously, the more you pay of the full price of the house originally, the less you will owe. If you invest $5,000 of your own in a $15,000 house, your monthly payments will be much less than if your down payment is only $2,000.

• *Interest rate.* While rates between lenders in any locality do not vary widely, one institution may charge half a percentage point less than another. Over a twenty-year period, this can amount to hundreds of dollars. It may add several dollars to what you will pay each month for the entire twenty-year period.

This table shows how the duration of your mortgage and the interest rate affect the amount you must pay each month on a $10,000 mortgage.

Duration	5¼%	5¾%	6%	6¼%	6½%
10 years	$108.50	$109.80	$111.00	$112.30	$113.50
12 years	95.00	96.30	97.60	98.90	100.20
15 years	81.70	83.00	84.40	85.70	87.10
20 years	68.80	70.20	71.70	73.10	74.50
25 years	61.40	62.90	64.40	66.00	67.50

• *Length of the mortgage.* Some institutions will not lend for longer than twenty years. Others will make loans for thirty years. The longer period of time you are given to pay off the mortgage, the less you will have to pay each month.

How these points work in actual practice is illustrated by the experiences of two men who worked side by side in an office. They earn the same weekly salary, and each has one child. The first man, with $1,500 saved, bought a $16,500 house with a $15,000 mortgage at 6 percent interest, which had to be paid off in fifteen years. He was stretching his credit to the breaking point. The other man had a $5,000 nest egg. He bought a $20,000 house, obtaining a $15,000 mortgage at 5 percent interest and with 25 years in which to pay it. He could carry his house comfortably. Here's the difference: The first man's monthly payment on the principal and interest amounted to $126.60; the second's was only $87.69.

How Amortized Mortgage Payments Work

If you take out an amortized, monthly-repayment home loan, you will be required to make a level or fixed payment each month during the life of the loan. The table below shows how your payment is applied and how your share of ownership in your home increases with each payment. At first, a relatively small part of your payment goes to pay off the principal, while interest charges are proportionately higher. As the loan is gradually repaid, the principal portion of each monthly payment becomes dominant while interest charges decrease.

This illustration below is based on a mortgage loan of $10,000 made for 20 years at 6% interest.

Can You Pass These FHA Requirements?

You won't want to spoil your chances of enjoying your home by assuming a debt too difficult to handle. So I consulted officials of the Federal Housing Administration to help you deter-

There Is an Art to Buying a House

Time		Monthly Payment		Principal Repayment	Balance Due on Loan at End of Month
Years	Months	Total	Interest Portion		
0	1	$71.70	$50.00	$21.70	$9,978.30
0	2	71.70	49.90	21.80	9,956.50
0	3	71.70	49.80	21.90	9,934.60
3	1	71.70	45.70	26.00	9,120.40
3	2	71.70	45.60	26.10	9,094.30
3	3	71.70	45.50	26.20	9,068.10
10	1	71.70	32.20	39.50	6,404.10
10	2	71.70	32.00	39.70	6,364.40
15	1	71.70	18.40	53.30	3,635.60
18	1	71.70	8.00	63.70	1,530.60
19	10	71.70	.90	70.80	116.10
19	11	71.70	.60	71.10	45.00
Final Payment		45.20	.20	45.00	0.00

—Source: United States Savings and Loan League

mine how much you can spend on housing each month without becoming a "bad risk." Here is how the F.H.A. itself would analyze your financial position in order to decide how much you could pay:

You must first estimate your "effective" income—the continuing income that you can rely on. You must also estimate your prospective monthly housing expense—what it will cost you to occupy the property. And then you must estimate all your debts, living costs, and other financial obligations. The F.H.A. explains why these estimates must be accurate:

• *"Your dependable income.* Since a long period of time is usually involved in paying off the mortgage obligation, the prospect of increasing your income above your regular salary is seldom a safe basis for determining the amount of housing expense you will be able to pay. A realistic estimate of your current dependable income is a sounder basis. In estimating dependable income, F.H.A. screens out all except income of a continuing nature.

"Income derived from overtime work, from employment of members of the family, from return from a capital investment, from the renting of a room, or from the rendering of occasional personal services can rarely be viewed as dependable, continuing income. Salaries of working wives may be considered effective for this purpose when their employment has been established as a part of the family life. Ordinarily it would not be reasonable to conclude that a wife's employment is a definite pattern of the life if she has married only a short time or had been employed only recently.

- *"Your housing expense.* There's more to housing expense than mortgage payments and taxes. Besides these items, housing expense generally includes hazard insurance premium, maintenance and repairs, utilities, etc.

"F.H.A. compares your prospective housing expense with the housing expense you are used to paying. If the prospective expense is greater and you have been unable to save any money while paying the smaller amount, there will be more risk in your undertaking the additional expense. The only way you could pay the increased amount, without having a corresponding increase in your income, would be to cut down on some of your other living expenses—and this is usually a very difficult thing to do.

- *"Your standard of living.* In arriving at a conclusion as to what is a safe relationship between your prospective housing expense and your net effective income, F.H.A. gives due consideration to the housing expense normal for your income bracket and to your use of installment credit as reflected in the items on your family budget.

- *"Your total financial obligations.* The relationship between your total financial obligations and your net effective income is extremely important to you as well as to the F.H.A.

"If the purchase of a certain home would mean you'd have

There Is an Art to Buying a House

to sacrifice too many other things to maintain a proper relationship, you might soon find home ownership becoming a burden rather than a pleasure to you, and if you were suddenly faced with financial reverses or an unexpected emergency it might even be necessary to sell your home at a loss.

"On the other hand, if there is a balanced relationship, where your income is sufficient to meet all your obligations without strain, the purchase of a home can bring lasting satisfaction to you and to your family.

"Experience gained from insuring mortgages on millions of homes in America has convinced the F.H.A. that no rule of thumb, no quick formula, can be indiscriminately applied in relating either housing expense or purchase price to a prospective home-owner's income.

"The only sure way of evaluating potential risk when you buy a home is to use good judgment—your own best judgment combined with the sound judgment furnished by experienced mortgage lenders and by the F.H.A."

To make this estimate of what you can pay for housing, first list your monthly income as follows:

1. WRITE DOWN YOUR MONTHLY INCOME.

    Your take-home pay $_____

    Wife's take-home pay $_____
    (If she is steadily employed)
    TOTAL INCOME $_____

2. LIST YOUR EXPENSES

    (a) LIVING EXPENSES (Monthly)

    Food $_____
    Clothing   _____
    Insurance premiums (fire, theft, liability, life, accident, hospital, etc.)   _____
    Education   _____
    Medical and dental   _____
    Automobile (operation, license, repairs)   _____
    Transportation   _____

Recreation and entertainment _____
Emergencies _____
Miscellaneous (dues, contributions, etc.) _____
                                    TOTAL $_____

(b) FIXED EXPENSES

Installment payments (automobile, appliances,
   furniture, etc.) $_____
Other debt payments (personal loans, etc.)   _____
State income taxes   _____
Retirement Fund   _____
Miscellaneous (support of parent, etc.)   _____
                                    TOTAL   _____
                                      (a)   _____
                                      (b)   _____
                           TOTAL EXPENSES $_____

3. SUBTRACT EXPENSES FROM INCOME

Total Monthly Income   _____
         Expenses   _____
Amount available for housing   _____

4. LIST MONTHLY HOUSING EXPENSES

Estimate Payment on Mortgage Loan:

   Principal $_____
   Interest   _____
   Insurance Premium (if F.H.A.)   _____
Hazard Insurance Premium   _____
Taxes and any special assessments   _____
Estimate for maintenance and repairs   _____

ESTIMATE FOR UTILITIES:

   Light   _____
   Heat   _____
   Water   _____
   Air Conditioning   _____
                                    TOTAL $_____

(Monthly Housing Expenses should not exceed amount available for housing.)

There Is an Art to Buying a House 151

Note that your sum of housing expenses should include what you must pay on your mortgage loan plus what it will cost you to keep up the house—utilities, maintenance and repairs, etc. You can get estimates of the cost of utilities from the local power company or builder (if you are buying a new house) or from the existing owner (if you are buying an older one).

How much should you allow annually for maintenance and repairs? While you cannot predict accurately what such costs will be, you can allow for a reasonable average. According to studies by the Allied Home Owners' Association of Roslyn, Long Island, a new home-buyer spends about $85 a year for this purpose during the first four years he owns the house, and $150 a year for the next six years. Repairs generally are negligible the first year but become necessary thereafter as minor flaws appear. For example, it may be necessary to paint where the wood trim has shrunk. During the third year, minor plumbing and electrical repairs may begin to be necessary. If the house is ten years old or older, allow about two percent of the total sales price to cover annual maintenance and repairs.

If you make this calculation before you begin to look for a house, you will be able to determine exactly the price range which best fits your circumstances.

Total Interest Cost

Of Amortized Mortgages for Various Loan Terms

The "easy" payments of the long-term mortgage loan are due to the reduced payments on the principal. But the borrower pays interest for so much longer that the total cost is much greater. It will pay you to consider the figures below showing how much more interest you must pay over the whole life of the loan as a result of "easier" terms.

$5,000 LOAN

Term of Loan	6%	5½%	5%
12 years	$ 2,027.20	$ 1,847.20	$ 1,660.00
20 years	3,604.00	3,256.00	2,920.00
15 years	2,596.00	2,362.00	2,119.00
25 years	4,675.00	4,225.00	3,775.00
30 years	5,800.00	5,224.00	4,666.00

$10,000 LOAN

12 years	$ 4,054.40	$ 3,694.40	$ 3,320.00
15 years	5,192.00	4,724.00	4,238.00
20 years	7,208.00	6,512.00	5,840.00
25 years	9,350.00	8,450.00	7,550.00
30 years	11,600.00	10,448.00	9,332.00

$15,000 LOAN

12 years	$ 6,081.60	$ 5,541.60	$ 4,980.00
15 years	7,788.00	7,086.00	6,357.00
20 years	10,812.00	9,768.00	8,760.00
25 years	14,025.00	12,675.00	11,325.00
30 years	17,400.00	15,672.00	13,998.00

What You Should Know About Mortgages

Almost everyone knows that buying a house is the greatest single investment the typical couple makes in a lifetime. And the amount of the mortgage loan which a savings and loan association, bank, insurance company, or other lending institution advances to help you pay the purchase price represents the largest sum you probably will ever borrow. Remember this important fact and you may save much money.

But you may not have much to say about the mortgage you will get. If you buy a new house, the builder may have arranged the mortgage terms before you entered the picture. If you buy an older house, it may have an existing mortgage which you are expected to continue. In either case, you probably could obtain a new mortgage, but the cost of "penalty charges" to terminate the old arrangement may be too much to make it worth while.

If you are building your own house—and sometimes if you are buying one already built—you'll be free to negotiate a new mortgage. If so, you can shop for one just as you'd shop for a car or appliance. You can explore for the best deal you can get.

Mr. Seiter explains:

Two basic kinds of mortgage are generally available at present. Both work on the monthly repayment principle. They are:

Government-insured mortgage. Under certain conditions the Federal Housing Administration or Veterans' Administration insure or guarantee that a bank or other lending institution will be protected if you fail to make your payments as specified. Thus the bank will recover part or all of any balance you are unable to pay.

F.H.A. loans require you—the borrower—to pay one-half of one percent of the amount you owe on your loan to cover the insurance cost each year. The insurance premium is included in the money payments to the bank. F.H.A. loans are available to any home-buyer. Of course, your credit standing must be good, and the house must pass F.H.A. construction tests.

V.A. Loans are available only to ex-members of the Armed Forces who qualify. The G.I.s do not pay the insurance fee directly. The V.A. loan program has been steadily declining in importance in recent years.

These federal programs encourage lending agencies to be more liberal than they would be ordinarily, since they are protected against loss. So you can usually obtain mortgages with lower down-payments and over longer periods than you might get otherwise.

There are several disadvantages to government-insured mortgages. The government rules are inflexible, and a lender who might be inclined to give you more favorable mortgage terms cannot do so because he must "follow the book." During periods when there is a shortage of money, the lender may find that he can lend for other purposes at higher rates than the

F.H.A. or V.A. permit him to charge. He may then be unwilling to write these mortgages. Funds available for you—the borrower—dry up.

Conventional mortgages. At almost any time, you can get a mortgage of this type. It is one the banker makes at his own risk. If money is scarce, the interest rates may be higher than those permitted on the government-insured mortgages. More often, lending institutions charge the same rate you would pay for interest and insurance under the F.H.A. plan. Sometimes you may even get a conventional mortgage at a lower rate.

Among the advantages of conventional loans is that the lender can use his own judgment as to the value of your property, based upon his intimate knowledge of local conditions. He can give you his decision whether he will grant a mortgage within a few days, instead of the few weeks generally required with government-sponsored mortgages. And there are fewer forms to fill out with a conventional-type loan.

Other desirable mortgage features, which you should get if you can, include:

• *Pre-payment clause.* Some lenders will let you pay off the face amount of the mortgage at any time without penalizing you. Others will allow you to pay off up to 20 percent of the outstanding loan each year without penalty. And others require that anyone who pays it all off ahead of time must pay six months' interest charges anyway. These penalties are exacted because the lender has gone to an expense to set up your mortgage, and does not want the added trouble and cost of investigating other places where he might lend the money. If you get a mortgage with a liberal pre-payment clause, you can reduce your debt at any time without paying for the privilege. Such pre-payment clauses are more common with conventional mortgages.

The opportunity to pay off your mortgage ahead of time is a valuable one to have, since it enables you to reduce your debt as you can and to increase your investment in your home. For

There Is an Art to Buying a House 155

example, if your income increases, you can add a certain amount to the stipulated sum you pay each month, and thus can own your home free and clear much faster.

• *"Open-end" feature.* When making an original mortgage, some lending institutions will agree to consider advancing you amounts in the future to improve the property, provided the total loan does not exceed the original amount of the mortgage. Suppose you buy a house with a $10,000 mortgage. After you have paid off $3,000, you decide to make bedrooms in your attic and a recreation room in your basement. A lender may advance up to the $3,000 to enable you to finance the work. If he agrees to the new loan, he will make it on the same terms as the original mortgage, saving you as much as seven percent interest annually on what you borrow. And you can space the extra payments over the life of the mortgage. The amount you have to pay each month will be only a small fraction of what it would be if you took out a standard two-year home-improvement loan. This feature also is more commonly found in conventional mortgages.

Don't Forget Your Closing Costs

John and Elizabeth Jones sat down to estimate what they could pay for a house. They finally decided that their $2,000 savings could be used for a down-payment and that John's salary could enable them to make the monthly payments and leave enough to live on. But after they signed the contract for the house, they discovered that they would have to pay an additional $500 in cash before they could move in. This unexpected sum came under the heading of closing costs—expenses involved in transferring the ownership of a house. Because they had overlooked closing costs, Mr. and Mrs. Jones spent a year trying to get out of the financial hole they had gone into.

Closing costs include:

Appraisers' fee (what the lender pays the expert who examines a house to determine its value. The lender must know this in order to know what amount to lend).

Expenses incurred in going through legal records to make certain that you will have a clear title to the property—that no one will show up later to claim it. Along with the fee for the title search, there will be a charge for title insurance which guarantees that the lender will not suffer a loss if an individual does show up to claim the property.

An engineer's survey of the house and lot to establish exactly where your property line lies in relation to the street and to lots on either side and in back of you.

Fees for recording the mortgage and the sale of the property, along with any revenue stamps and notary's charges.

Premiums on fire insurance carried on the house. The lender requires this so that its investment will be protected if a fire or other accident damages the property. (It requires only enough insurance to cover the mortgage. Make sure that you have enough to protect your investment as well.)

Closing costs depend upon the cost of the property involved and other factors. Before you sign to buy a house, ask the lending agency to tell you what these costs will be. If you let them take you by surprise, you may get an unpleasant shock as did the Joneses.

In addition to closing costs, don't forget that you will have your lawyer's fee to pay as well. Before engaging him, don't hesitate to ask what it will be. It may amount to as much as one percent of the cost of the house. He may expect to be paid during the "closing ceremony," when you officially take possession.

Closing costs and legal fees are one good reason why you should think twice before choosing a house. If you become dissatisfied after you buy and want to pull up stakes and go elsewhere, you'll have little chance of recovering the amount you have laid out for these costs—and you'll face more closing costs with your new house.

Four Musts to Help You Choose the Right House

Herman H. York of Jamaica, N.Y., easily qualifies as one of America's outstanding home architects. Since World War II, more than 100,000 homes in all parts of the country have been built from his plans. Mr. York is a member of the American Institute of Architects and a consultant to the National Association of Home Builders. I asked him to outline the important rules every home-buyer must remember in order to make a sound purchase. He cites four fundamental principles. They are:

• *Thoroughly investigate the neighborhood.* It can make or mar your satisfaction with your home, and will determine whether or not you will be happy with your purchase. Investigating the neighborhood means more than merely driving around. You must consider how community factors will affect your living conditions throughout the year. Ask yourself: How will you get to church and stores? How will your children get to school? If they must walk, will the roads be in good condition after a heavy rain? Or will they be up to their knees in mud? If your car is laid up, will you be able to get to at least some shops to buy necessities?

The following examples indicate why a thorough investigation of the neighborhood is necessary:

One couple saw a bargain-priced old house in October and agreed to buy it. In May, cars began parking on their lawn. Blazing lights, blaring bands and roaring crowds kept them awake until past midnight every night. A baseball park was a block and a half away.

A family bought a house in Westchester County, N. Y. and counted on a nearby bus line for transportation. It worked fine weekdays, but they were home-bound weekends: The bus ran only five days a week.

After a peace-loving woman moved into a development near

Los Angeles, she found a neighborhood feud raging. Half the residents don't speak to the other half. If she chats with her neighbor on the right, the neighbor on the left snubs her for weeks, and vice versa.

Farmlands in one section of Ohio mushroomed with houses overnight. A little village is the only place for hundreds of families to shop. Now they spend half their Saturdays looking for parking space.

• *Analyze the house in terms of your family's needs.* The perfect house for one family will be entirely wrong for another. Recently a national home-builders' magazine gave a prize in a contest to an architect who designed a home with one bedroom—and with one bathroom which could be reached only through the bedroom. This house was suitable for a man and wife without children who did little entertaining and therefore had no concern about bathroom facilities for guests. But 90 percent of American couples would find the design intolerable.

You will want to consider your family's present size and the possibility that you will have more children later. In fact, failure to plan for the needs of a larger family is the commonest mistake young couples make. In a typical case, a G.I. and his bride found a two-bedroom cottage, signed the papers and moved in. The house was huge at first. Then children arrived. The family needed more bedrooms but the cottage provided no way to get them. By then, the family had thousands of dollars invested and strong roots in the neighborhood. But they had to pull up stakes, losing money on the house.

Two-bedroom houses without expansion attics went up by the millions after World War II. Now in many sections they are hard to sell. Buyers have become aware of the fact that adding an expansion attic while the house is under construction costs only a few hundred dollars—but gives them room to grow in.

The arrangement of rooms is another important factor to

There Is an Art to Buying a House

consider. Suppose you have small children, and buy a two-story home with all the bedrooms upstairs. A youngster becomes ill. You will be run ragged climbing stairs. Likewise, if you lack a bathroom near your back door, your youngsters may drag mud all over the house in order to reach one. If your living room is a traffic room—one you must pass through to get from one room to another—you will find it difficult to keep clean. If you can't reach your garage without getting soaked when it rains or snows, it may prove mighty annoying.

Here are other flaws which would make your house less convenient:

Poorly-planned kitchen. A housewife works in this room more than any other. It should be near living and dining rooms to save her steps. It should enable a mother to see her children playing in the yard. Appliances should be arranged so that work proceeds easily from refrigerator to sink to range, with counter space alongside each. There should be adequate storage space; with enough shelves to store food, you can save substantially both in time and money. You need not make so many trips to the food stores, thus cutting car expenses. And you will be able to stock up on items on sale.

Noisy sleeping area. Young children may be kept awake late at night because of insufficient noise barriers between bedroom and living room or recreation room, where the TV sets or radio may be on while guests are being entertained. Look for bedrooms separated from the living room either by closets which make excellent noise barriers because they trap air, or by a hall, bathroom, or by an insulated ceiling or floor.

Inadequate floor space. Modern families have more possessions than ever before, and they need more space to store them. With your growing family you'll need space for a baby carriage, children's furniture, bike, sleds, out-of-season sports equipment, etc. Many authorities agree that the basement offers the lowest-cost storage space in the home. A full basement gives you almost as much floor space as your entire first floor and can be used not only for storage but also for a recreation room, workshop, or hobby room and laundry. You'll find your basement doubly useful for all purposes if it has its own exit to the outdoors. Then youngsters and others can use it freely without disturbing other members of the family. If the house does not have a basement, double-check its storage space.

Other desirable features include adequate space for outdoor living where you can relax comfortably when the weather is good; adequate bathroom facilities—one on each floor, preferably two in a three-bedroom house; a garage near the kitchen, enabling you to bring groceries from car to pantry without getting soaked on rainy days; a back entrance where you can drop your umbrellas and boots to avoid tracking mud over your front hall; adequate wall space for the furniture you now own; large enough electrical service to handle all your appliances.

If you plan to have a house built for you, and will have no chance to see the finished building before you commit yourself, you can visualize whether it will have the above conveniences by carefully studying the floor plan.

• *Don't over-buy for the neighborhood.* Every section has a set character. One has high-cost homes with beautiful, well-kept lawns. Another has homes in the lowest-price range. Buy or build a house that costs twice as much as the average in either community, and you'll probably never be able to sell it for what you paid.

It is a well-known fact that home values, like water, tend to seek their own level. People who can afford a $30,000 house prefer to associate with others who earn about the same as they do. They are reluctant to buy where their neighbors earn only half as much.

You generally will be better off financially in buying a house that is below the average price of the other homes in the community. Their higher value will tend to pull up the value of your house. However, your house should not be so much cheaper that it would be conspicuous: When you tried to sell, prospects would fear your neighbors would look down on them.

Keeping your house within the prevailing price-range of your neighborhood is also a good point to remember if you are tempted to undertake an expensive remodelling project after you move in. One horrible example: A New Jersey couple bought a $12,000 house in a section of $12,000 houses. A year later, the wife inherited a large sum and the couple went on an improvement spree. They added rooms in back and on one side, ripped out the old kitchen and installed all new equipment, and added two bathrooms. Before long, they had $20,000 invested. Then the husband was offered a better job in another town and they had to sell. The most they could get was $15,500.

• *Hire an expert to check on the construction.* Your mortgage company will gladly recommend an experienced appraiser. For about $35, he will carefully examine the house you're interested in, uncover its hidden defects if any and tell you what it's really worth. If you try to scrimp on this detail, you may get stuck for a hundred times his fee.

A young couple saw their dream house on a wooded lot. "Three others are interested in this beauty, so you'd better act fast if you want it," the salesman told them, so they wrote a check without consulting anyone. They moved in, congratulating themselves on their shrewdness. Then their new neighbors told them that the house had been on the market for months. Half a dozen times before, it had looked as if a deal was set; then prospects brought experts around, who noted that the place was crawling with termites.

Generally, most of your questions can be answered by the lending institution, but many people have a lawyer represent them when they buy.

Once you have decided that you would be happier in your own home, and have decided what you can afford to pay and what features you want your house to have, you will have to make several additional decisions. You will have to decide whether to buy an old house or new, whether to build your own house, whether to buy a prefabricated house. These questions will be discussed in the next chapter.

chapter ten

WHAT KIND OF HOUSE IS BEST FOR YOU?

An old home may be a better buy for you. Or maybe you would prefer a development house, a prefab or a trailer

Suppose you have decided that your family will face a brighter future in a home you can call your own. Should you buy an old house or a new one? There are pros and cons for each. You will have to consider the advantages and disadvantages of each type, then make up your mind in accordance with your own circumstances and tastes.

The older house often offers a better buy. A survey I made of real estate brokers revealed these reasons:

• *The older house usually provides more space for your money.* The typical home-buyer today wants as much room as he can get. His family is larger and his home is the center of family activities to a greater extent than it was a few years ago. And the cost per square foot of floor space in older homes often is only half what you'd have to pay for it in a new home.

• *Your house is ready to live in.* The typical buyer of a new home must put in his own lawn and landscaping. What seems at first like an easy job can easily amount to hundreds of dollars for peat moss, fertilizer and grass seed alone. He may need screens, storm doors and storm windows; sunken garbage pails, closet shelves, walks around the sides of the house, perhaps even a driveway. All these things are likely to be installed in an older house.

- *It's easier to examine the house and the neighborhood.* The building's short-comings—uneven floors, wall and ceiling cracks due to settlement—will be apparent. It probably is located in an established neighborhood, so that you can carefully examine what's on the next block, where the bus line runs, how far you'd be from shops, schools, churches, what kind of youngsters yours will play with.
- *Tax rates will probably be more stable.* In older communities, little or no room generally is left for new houses. Schools, police and fire departments have already been set up and are not likely to be expanded. So you won't be hit with sudden, sharp increases in taxes.
- *You often can bargain for a lower price.* You generally deal with an individual who wishes to sell quickly. If he has held the house even a few years, he probably will seek more than he paid. If you offer less than his price, you don't ask him to take a loss but merely to reduce his profit—something he'll find easier to do.

Buying an older house, however, generally involves drawbacks, too. For instance:

- *You may have to be satisfied with an old-fashioned design.* Styles in houses change like those in cars, and one built 25 years ago generally won't look as attractive as one erected today. Some equipment—kitchen cabinets, bath fixtures, etc.—may be out-of-date. Your garage may be too small even for a compact car.
- *Your house may be in a "declining neighborhood."* For about fifteen years after the first homes are built in a typical community, the neighborhood tends to rise. Its appearance is being improved by landscaping, additions, and so on. For another ten years or so, the community tends to stay on a level. After that, unless the home-owners spend more time and money on maintaining their property, the tendency may be for the neighborhood to decline. Owners who have neglected repair jobs may have made their homes permanent blots on the neigh-

borhood. Property values all around them may begin to go down.

• *It may be harder to form friendships.* Home-owners in an old neighborhood probably have many existing friends there, and won't be very interested in you. You're likely to get a cold shoulder from them. If most of the existing home-owners are elderly—a common condition in sections settled fifteen or more years before—your own youngsters may not have anyone to play with.

• *You'll probably have maintenance problems from the very beginning.* Plumbing, heating, wiring, are more likely to need repairs or replacement. You'll have to fight a constant battle against encroaching obsolescence.

• *You may need a higher down-payment.* Lenders usually won't lend as much proportionately on an old house as on a new one.

Advantages of older houses generally are the disadvantages of new ones, and vice versa. Few builders erect a house without a buyer, but get the buyer and then build the house. Therefore, you're unlikely to see your new house before you agree to buy it. To a small extent, at least, you will be buying a pig in a poke. In fact, officials of Better Business Bureaus in all parts of the country report that blind buying of new houses is a major source of the complaints they receive.

Nevertheless, purchasing a new house affords many plus factors:

You may get by with a lower down-payment. It may be as little as 10 percent of the sales price if the house costs $15,000 or less, 15 percent on houses up to $20,000, and 20 percent on homes up to $30,000.

You'll probably have a bright, clean home with few maintenance problems for three years or more.

You'll find it much easier to make friends where everyone else is also a new home-buyer and has many of your own problems.

For a few years at least, and probably longer, houses comparable to yours will more than likely bring higher prices than they cost originally.

If You Buy a New House—

There are several different ways of buying a new house:

• *You can buy one already built.* Builders occasionally erect a house without a buyer in sight. After it is completed, they offer it for sale. You can use all the checks recommended for buying an old house. You can examine the construction, see how the building fits into the terrain, inspect the finished kitchen, judge the neighborhood, and so on. Main disadvantage is that you have nothing to say about how the house is built or its basic features; you take what you get. And since the builder worked on a speculative basis, using his own funds, he probably wants a larger profit than he'd expect if he were sure from the onset of construction that the house would be sold. Sometimes the builder arranges for the mortgage in these cases; sometimes the buyer does.

• *You can have one "custom-built" to your specifications.* You can buy your own lot, hire an architect to draw plans for the exact house you want, then select a builder. This is the most expensive way to build. An architect may charge from a few hundred to a few thousand dollars for the plans, depending upon how much work he must do to translate your dreams onto blueprints. For an extra fee (up to five percent of the total cost of the house) he will also supervise its construction.

The advantage of having a house built to your own specifications is obvious: You will get what you want. However, the cost may be too much for you. Building this way has become possible only for those with upper-bracket incomes.

If you build in this way, hire a competent architect who is experienced in designing homes. Many do most of their work drawing plans for factories and stores and are not familiar with the latest design ideas for homes and the actual needs of young families with children.

Make sure to get at least three estimates from reputable contractors. Before letting out any contract, check the lowest bidder's references personally and assure yourself of his financial responsibility. Ask your banker whether you should have the contractor bonded so that the house can be completed without loss to you even if he goes bankrupt or leaves town. See that he carries liability insurance so that if a workman is injured on the job, you will not be held personally responsible.

Also call in an experienced lawyer to help you draw up your contract with the builder. By putting down in writing everything you expect to get, he will help you avoid future arguments with contractors—a common occurrence when houses are built this way. You will have to arrange for any mortgage yourself.

• *You can buy a "development house."* Almost all large-scale builders in the United States are "tract" or "development" builders who erect whole colonies of houses in one section. Three out of every five homes built at present go up in developments where there are a dozen or more similar houses.

Usually the builder erects and furnishes a sample house and then invites prospects to inspect it. You see a house almost identical to the one which he offers to erect for you on a different plot. This method has some of the advantages of buying a completed house, since you can easily visualize the features of the home you would get. It also has some advantages of "custom building," since the builder usually will add features you prefer to the house he will erect for you. Because of the economies possible with mass production, developments generally give the most for the money in new housing.

Remember, however, that the "model" merely represents a house *like* the one you get. The land on which your house will be built will have different problems from the one on which the model was built. It may be on a sloping lot, not a flat one. It may be planted in the middle of an underground stream or a section with a high water table, and the foundation that resists water on the site of the model house might not do so here. It may be in a section with an entirely different view. All these factors will make your house different.

Nor does the fact that you see a finished house mean that you should not carefully examine how it was built. You should find out what materials were used behind the walls, for what you can't see may affect how comfortable and maintenance-free the house will be. For example, how thick is the insulation? If mineral wool, it should be at least two inches thick in the walls, four inches thick in the ceiling. If the wall material is gypsum board, what thickness is it? In reasonably good construction, a half-inch thickness is used on walls, ⅜th-inch or half-inch thickness in ceilings. Thinner wallboard might not resist the punishment young children could give. Is the electrical wiring adequate for present and expected future needs? It is if the fuse-box or circuit-breaker indicates that the house has 100 ampere, three-wire or 220-volt service.

Because model houses often are furnished and filled with appliances to make them look more attractive, try to determine exactly what you will and won't get for the price quoted you. For instance, you may not get the gleaming refrigerator, dishwasher or garbage disposal unit shown in the kitchen, nor the clothes-washer and dryer in the laundry. Instead of the magnificent wallpaper in the demonstration model, you may be limited to one or two colors of paint and wallpaper costing $1 or less a roll; for anything better you will have to pay extra.

Although the house sanitary system will be hooked into a community sewer, an extra assessment may be levied on the home-owner. But the builder may not tell you this unless you ask. The lawn and landscaping around the model house may be beautiful. Will you get the same? Probably not; a clause in the purchase contract may allow you $75 worth of work, a mere fraction of what good grass and shrubs would cost.

The mortgage you can get on a development house is a good indication of what lenders think it's worth. If you need only a small down-payment and can extend payments over a thirty-year period, a mortgage institution obviously believes the house is well worth its price and that it will be able to get its money back if you fail to make your payments and it must sell over your head.

Development builders generally arrange for one lending institution to take mortgages for all the houses in their tract. They shop for the best terms. In fact, some spend more time arranging mortgages for their houses than any other detail. You benefit in lower interest rates and other favorable features. However, you are generally required to take the mortgage the builder has obtained. If you want a different mortgage, or pay cash to avoid having any mortgage at all, it may cost several hundred dollars to get out of the contract he has made.

Prefabricated houses are usually erected by builders in tracts, and the principles involved in choosing a prefab are the same as those recommended for buying any development house. Prefabs merely are made differently. Their wall, floor, ceiling and roof surfaces often are put together at a factory, then shipped to the site where they are assembled on the foundation prepared for them. On the other hand, all construction work for conventionally-built houses generally is done on the spot. But when a prefab stands alongside one erected in the older way, even an expert might find it difficult to tell which is which.

• *You can be your own builder.* Larry Eisinger is one of the foremost authorities on do-it-yourself home building in America. He built his beautiful home on Staten Island, N. Y., with his own hands, is the author of the book, "How to Build and Contract Your Own Home," and as editor-in-chief of Fawcett Books, New York, he has supervised the writing and editing of several hundred books dealing with all phases of home construction, repair and maintenance.

This is what Mr. Eisinger says:

"A professional contractor may expect to take up to 20 percent of the total cost of the house as his profit, depending upon the price of the house and the local competitive situation. While he has access to sources of labor and materials which may not be available to you, you can save a substantial part of his profit by handling the administrative details. To do this successfully, you need initiative, common sense, and some basic understanding of house construction, although you will not need as much technical knowledge as you might imagine. Hundreds of thousands of Americans have built their own homes successfully.

"You will have to obtain your building plans from a local architect or direct mail plan service and submit them for approval by your local building department. You will also have to submit them to a bank with a list of materials to be used, if you wish to get a loan to help you finance the construction. It will be your job to buy the lumber and other materials and to negotiate with subcontractors—masons who will erect your foundation, carpenters, plumbers, heating-men, electricians, painters, and so on. You will have to see that their work is done on schedule and you will have to arrange for periodic inspections by the community building inspector and a representative of the bank which has agreed to underwrite your mortgage.

"In addition to saving money, when you are your own contractor, you retain control over the building process. You're sure of what you're getting because you watch intimately each stage of construction. Therefore you're better able to see what is going into your house. If you're a competent administrator and know how to shop for labor and materials, you may be able to make extra savings.

"Disadvantages are that you must devote a great deal of

your time to this project. For the amount of time involved, perhaps you could earn more in your own line of work. If the house costs more than the amount you estimated, you stand to lose; if you hired a builder, this extra amount would come out of his expected profit. However, the danger of getting stuck this way is not so great as most people think. If you select your contractors carefully, shop for prices, and heed the advice of your banker, building supply dealer, and persons who have put up their own homes, and also consult the excellent books on this subject, you'll find that building your own home can give you satisfactions which those who merely buy one don't know."

• *You can do some or most of the work yourself.* "Hundreds of firms throughout the country exist to provide materials for individuals who want to put their own physical labor into their houses," Mr. Eisinger states. "If you do some or most of the work, you'll not only be the general contractor, but also a sub-contractor responsible for various aspects of the completed project. Of course, your chance to save money is greater.

"Some firms will sell you a 'shell'—the foundation floors, walls and roof, and will erect it on your property. You can do the finishing work—plumbing, heating, wiring, painting, etc., or you can hire contractors for those jobs you don't want to do. Other firms will sell you pre-cut houses with all the lumber cut to exact size. You merely nail all the piece together.

"Many local lumber merchants who are members of the Lumber Retailers' Association will also cut to size all the lumber you need for your house. They often will recommend a local contractor you can hire to do the work, or will show you how you can do it for yourself. Men without previous carpentry experience have erected sound, attractive homes in this way. You can also buy the rough lumber and cut it to size yourself, thus saving on what lumber yards or pre-cut house manufacturers must charge, but also increasing the possibility of costly errors.

"Probably few 'do-it-yourself' home-builders actually do all the work. They find it more desirable to give out those jobs for which they lack experience, training or confidence, which require strenuous physical effort (concrete or masonry work, for instance), or those that require licensed craftsmen, such as plumbing and electrical work. What jobs can the ordinary man perform? It is generally agreed that no special talent is required to install insulation, to put down resilient floor tile, to install a lawn, or to put factory-made kitchen cabinets in place. Any man can do rough carpentry work—nailing the rough sub-floor to floor joists, for instance—because any mistakes will not be seen after the finished floor is laid.

"On the other hand, certain skills are required for electrical wiring, to install water supply and waste disposal lines and plumbing equipment, or to put in the heating system. Before you try to do your own wiring, plumbing or heating work, even if you feel qualified to do so, make certain that your local community permits it. Local laws sometimes require that such work be done only by licensed tradesmen.

"If you are building your own home, make mortgage arrangements before you excavate. If your plans are O.K. and your credit is good, the bank's mortgage officer will arrange to lend you money at various stages of construction.

"Let's assume that he agrees to lend $20,000 on the completed house. He may agree to give you one quarter—$5,000—at each of the following stages:

"1. When the carpenters have completely enclosed the house, with the roof in place.

"2. When interior partitions are in place and plumbing, heating and electrical lines have been installed.

"3. When interior walls and bathroom tile are installed, kitchen cabinets and counter-tops are in place, and finished flooring is laid.

"4. When your house is fully painted, all other details have

What Kind of House Is Best for You?

been attended to, and you have received a certificate of occupancy from your building department which states that the house is safe to live in.

"You will find your building loan an aid when dealing with your sub-contractors. If the inspector is dissatisfied with the quality of work done, he will refuse to make your payment until the defects have been remedied. You can therefore tell your sub-contractor that you can't pay until his job is satisfactory."

Two Rules to Help You Buy a Lot Wisely

Buying a lot can be as important as your choice of a house to build on it. That's because buying a lot commits you to a neighborhood—to schools, churches, shops and dozens of other characteristics of a community. Many real estate experts hold that an inferior house in a good neighborhood usually is much more valuable than a good house in poor surroundings. One dramatic example: A builder erected rows of identical houses in two different sections of Long Island. Those in an attractive community sold quickly for $15,000. The same houses in poor settings were priced $2,000 lower, yet did not sell as well. Conclusion? You may lose a great deal by buying a "bargain lot," because its defects may seriously impair the value of any house you put on it. Every lot-buyer should observe two basic points:

• *Buy only when you are ready to build.* Several real estate brokers have advised me that buying a lot in the hope of building in several years, or of making a profit by re-selling it, generally proves to be a mistake. Here is why:

An empty lot is an expensive thing to hold. First, figure the value of your time in selecting and negotiating for the lot. The money you pay would be drawing interest if invested elsewhere, so you must figure the loss of interest as part of the cost. In addition, you must pay taxes every year, and perhaps assessments for sewers, roads, and so on.

If you hold an empty lot, its actual cost in three years may total 50 percent more than you paid originally. Because of these factors, you might buy a lot today and sell it in five years at double the price—yet still lose money.

Another important consideration is that your tastes may change. You may buy a lot today, thinking you'd like to build a split-level house, with one side higher than the other. After a few years, you may change your mind and want a ranch house with all the rooms on one floor. The lot you bought for the first type may be unfitted for the other.

Your own circumstances may also change. Today you may be childless and earning $6,000 a year. In three years you may have two children and your income may be $10,000. A house that fits your needs when you buy a lot might seem unsuitable later.

While you are waiting to build, the community may also change radically. For example, a rural section that seems like an ideal place for a home may be carved up within a few years. You may find a superhighway running past your block, a factory down the street, or a new development nearby with lots of children who push the school tax sky-high. What seemed ideal when you bought the lot may become the type of section that you no longer wish to live in.

True, these things could also happen if you built a house at once, but at least you would get some benefit from your property. Moreover, as a resident you would be more alert to what was going on in your community, and better able to prevent it in your local government.

If you buy land from a developer at so much down and so much per month, he may mortgage the lot until you make your final payment. As a result of many sad experiences by land purchasers, the Better Business Bureau of Baltimore warns that the developer may go bankrupt or leave town while the mortgage is in effect. The mortgage-holder may then take possession of the land—leaving you out in the cold.

• *Examine the lot personally, and with the utmost care.* This point is emphasized by Robert Frese, assistant vice president in charge of mortgages for the Dime Savings Bank of Brooklyn, one of the largest investors in home mortgages in the East. Difficult as it is to believe, thousands of lots are bought each week by persons who have never been within hundreds of miles of them: The selling of lots by mail, mainly in the $10 down, $10 a week category, has become a major industry. Huge colonies in Florida, Arizona, the desert areas of Southern California and elsewhere have been promoted in this way.

Many mail order developers are legitimate, but the most honest of them do not know exactly what you want in a lot, and your chances of getting stuck with undesirable property are magnified when you buy in this way.

Here are Mr. Frese's recommendations:

1. Never agree to buy a building lot until you have investigated thoroughly. Personally check how close you will be to community churches, shops. Go to the city or town hall and find out whether the section you are considering is residentially zoned to prevent construction of factories, stores, apartment houses or other undesirable buildings. Make sure that there won't be any provisions in the deed to the land that may prevent you from building the type of house you wish. For example, some communities prohibit any but two-story houses. Another community may require you to build a larger house than you want.

2. Ask the local tax collector what the taxes will be for the lot and the house you expect to build. Don't take the land salesman's word for it or you may find your annual tax bill hundreds of dollars higher than you expected. Get local bus

and train schedules. Find out how the fares compare with those of communities nearby. If they are low, look for a fare increase later.

3. When you are satisfied with neighborhood conditions, turn your attention back to the lot and examine it carefully. Don't be satisfied if a salesman tells you it is a "quarter-acre" or "half-acre." Demand to know the exact length, width and depth. From the town building department, learn the regulations affecting "set-backs." Many communities require that houses be built certain distances from the front, sides and back of the lot. In one town, all structures must be more than thirty feet from the front line of the lot, 25 feet from the rear, and more than 8 feet from either side. Therefore, if you buy a 50 by 80-foot lot in that town, your house would have to be less than 25 feet deep or 32 feet long—little more than a cottage.

4. Think twice if the lot has a sharp slope. If so, you may have to build a split-level house to fit the contour of the ground or spend a small fortune for dirt to make the lot reasonably level around the sides of a one-story or two-story house. And your children may not have a level play space in the yard.

5. Determine what soil conditions prevail. If neighbors live nearby, ask them if water enters their basements or if the ground is rocky. In either case, building on your lot may be prohibitively costly.

6. Find out how house sewage is disposed of. If street sewers are in place, you will have the best possible disposal system. If not, you may have to pay to install a sewer later, so check whether the community installs sewers out of the general funds or assesses individual home-owners who are thus served. If no sewers are available, you will have to use septic tank or cesspools which enable the waste from the house to sink into the soil. Make sure the soil is porous enough to accommodate this type of disposal. If a private well must be dug, the sanitary facilities should be sufficient distance from the well to prevent pollution.

7. Also ascertain whether water and electricity will be available. If you can't get town water, you will have to dig a well on your property. Ask neighbors what they paid for their wells, so that you will have an idea of what yours would cost. Since well-diggers customarily charge so much for each foot down they go to reach water, a deep well may cost many hundreds of dollars. Electricity is available in most places, but if lines cannot easily be strung to your house, the utility company may charge extra to set up wires to serve you. Better check this, or find out what it would cost for a generator to provide your own electricity.

If you follow Mr. Frese's suggestions, investigate the lot thoroughly and double-check all claims made by the lot salesman, you'll avoid the errors which often result later in disgruntled lot-owners. You won't be like the couple who bought a $1,500 lot in a "lake front development" sight unseen. When they finally went to examine the lot, they discovered it partly under water—and the "lake" was less than three feet deep and infested with mosquitoes. Nor will you be like the couple who bought an Arizona lot by mail, dreaming of a quiet place where they could lie outdoors and soak up the sunshine. They had the lot half paid for before they inspected it. They found it alongside a main highway; their outdoor living would consist of smelling the fumes of huge diesel-burning trucks that roared past day and night.

How much should you pay for the lot in proportion to the cost of the house you plan? Here is one popular, workable formula:

First determine the total cost of the lot with improvements. This total should include the cost of the lot itself, cost of a well if you must dig one, cost of a septic tank or cesspool if one will be needed, amount of any sewer assessment you will have to pay to use the town sewage system, and also the cost (if any) of paved streets in front of your property. The result you get will give you the cost of a completely improved lot.

This cost should roughly equal one-fourth of what the house will cost, or one-fifth of what the house and lot together will cost. If the lot costs more than one-third of the cost of the house, chances are that the house will be a wall-flower—too poor for the community. If the lot costs less than one-sixth of the house, it probably will be expensive for the neighborhood.

The National Better Business Bureau adds this caution: personally check current selling prices of other land in the immediate area of your lot. It explains: "Individual lots in some promotions have sometimes been offered at prices many times higher than the price of other available land in the immediate vicinity.

"In order to avoid the danger that your payment in the property may be jeopardized because of liens, judgments, or unpaid taxes, make sure that the title to the property is searched thoroughly before you pay any money.

"If you are asked to pay so much down and so much a month over a period of time, make sure that you thoroughly understand all the details of the arrangements. Get a copy of the contract or bill of sale ahead of time, and study it carefully or ask your lawyer to do so.

"If a down-payment is required, discuss with your attorney the advisability of placing such payment in escrow. Are the terms of the contract subject to your ability to obtain the satisfactory mortgage from a lender of your choosing? This point is important, because you should know whether you can obtain a mortgage and whether there is an existing mortgage on the property. If so, must the buyer assume the mortgage, or will the seller satisfy the mortgage and discharge its lien? What are the alternatives? How much are the closing costs? Can they be included in the mortgage? If there is no mortgage, what are the carrying charges, if any, on the unpaid balance?

"It is advisable to check all arrangements with your attorney and to retain an attorney for arranging and closing the full transaction."

Start with a Trailer Home?

If you lack the down-payment for a home, yet want your own place, and if a trailer park is near where you work, consider living in a trailer for several years.

Advantages of life in a trailer—or "mobile home," the term manufacturers prefer—are mostly economic. Spokesmen of the Mobile Homes Manufacturers' Association told me that for about $2,000 you can buy a model that is fully equipped with furniture, kitchen appliances, and bathroom and will sleep four persons. Luxurious models, with three bedrooms, two bathrooms and 500 square feet of floor space, may run as high as $7500.

For about $4,000 you can obtain a trailer which will provide the space and furnishings for which you would have to pay perhaps $150 a month in a city apartment. Moreover, maintenance costs of a trailer are low, and you can rent space in many trailer parks for $30, gas and electricity included. So by living in a mobile home you can save a large sum on rent and housing over a period of several years.

Most lenders will now advance the money to buy a mobile home as easily as if you were buying a car. Generally, you pay a quarter of the price down, and part of the remainder each month for periods up to seven years. After you have the trailer paid off, it may have a resale value equalling half the original cost. If you put aside each month the difference between your monthly trailer costs and what it would cost to rent an apartment, you soon may have enough saved to make a substantial down-payment on a home.

Of course, not everyone enjoys this kind of life. You may not have much space around your mobile home and may have even less privacy than in an apartment. Unless you enjoy being very neighborly, the necessity of living so close to others may depress you.

Some persons dislike the "cooped-up" feeling they say they get in a trailer. There generally is a shortage of closet space and of space for large-scale entertaining. Sometimes no more than five or six persons can be accommodated inside at one time. Some mobile home settlements are located in less attractive sections; you may have to live behind a gas station, or off the main highway on which trucks roar past day and night.

An advantage is that you can move your mobile home whenever you wish. However, most dwellers in mobile home camps remain in one parking spot longer than six months and 40 percent stay longer than a year. Entertainers, resort workers, salesmen and others whose jobs require moving about the country find this kind of housing ideal for their purposes.

chapter eleven

DOES YOUR FAMILY REALLY NEED A SECOND INCOME?

How to figure if it is worth it when a husband "moonlights" or a wife works outside the home

Most readers who have followed the suggestions in this book will have no difficulty in living within their incomes with savings left over. But when many families find that their spending exceeds income, they try to balance the scale in another way—by increasing income. The additional money may be earned by "moonlighting"—a job held by the main breadwinner after his regular working hours—or by his wife in a full or part-time job.

Second jobs are held by an estimated 2,500,000 men. Because of the 35-hour work week, many can take part-time jobs without working any longer per week than everyone did around the turn of the century. Many also take second jobs that serve as recreation. A factory worker who is handy with tools does home repairs in his spare time, earns $30 a week, and has fun doing it. A high school teacher sells real estate evenings and week-ends. He marks test papers and prepares his lessons while he waits for clients. A shoe salesman who is interested in automobiles works Saturdays at a gas station.

According to a survey by the United States Department of Labor, most wives who take outside jobs do so to support themselves, to contribute to family living expenses, to help buy a house, or help pay for their children's education. About 24,000,000 women are now in the labor force.

Many authorities question whether it is really worthwhile for wives to work or for husbands to take second jobs. For example, psychologists seem to agree that a child needs his mother's personal care during his formative years and may suffer serious harm without her. Likewise, they say, a father should serve as a model of manhood—to give his boys an example of how to act in the adult situations they will face, and his girls an understanding of how to deal with men. In many cases, therefore, the family's extra income probably is not worth the emotional harm which is done.

Does It Pay to Take a Second Job?

Most authorities agree that before any family decides that financial problems can be solved by a wife taking an outside job, or by a husband taking a second one, these five questions should be answered:

1. Will It Pay to Take a Second Job? For every additional dollar you earn, your tax rate will be proportionately higher. Suppose the federal tax rate on one income reaches 22 percent. Of every extra dollar you earn, you will keep only 78 cents or less. In addition, there may be state income taxes to pay, and there will be deductions for Social Security and state unemployment taxes.

There may be extra expenses in connection with the second job. These include costs of traveling to and from work, extra union dues and fees, etc. It may be customary to take one or more coffee-breaks. There may be collections when a fellow employee gets married, has a baby, becomes ill or dies. You may think you have to eat lunch at more expensive places than you would ordinarily choose, to have drinks with fellow-employees after work, to do more entertaining at home.

Working women generally need more clothing and beauty

treatments than do housewives. Working mothers may spend a good part of their earnings on baby-sitters or maids to care for their children while they are away. Or they may spend more on transportation and phone calls, trying to coordinate their schedules as parents and employees.

One survey by economists of the Department of Agriculture indicated that less than half of every dollar that a working wife sees on her pay-check is actually added to the family income. This survey showed that the average wife earned $2,200 a year. She paid $614 for transportation, lunches, and other items. She paid $184 for laundry and for baby-sitters. Personal grooming and clothing, otherwise unnecessary, cost $105. Even without taxes, she had only $1,297 to show on income which was supposed to be $2,200.

You can use a quick method to determine whether it will really pay a husband to "moonlight" or a wife to work outside the home.

First, list all expenses that the job entails—transportation, extra meals, clothing, etc. Estimate costs for baby-sitters, laundry services, household repairs and other extras which you must now pay for. Make your estimates high, rather than low. The average family under-estimates them. Deduct all these expenses from your stated wages.

Now list the extra income you will get Determine what income tax bracket you are in—the highest percentage you must pay on your first income. (Married tax-payers who file a joint return and have a taxable income of $4,000 or less pay 20 percent. As your taxable income increases, the tax rate on the additional amount also increases.) To your tax percentage, add about five percent more—a rough estimate to cover Social Security and withholding unemployment insurance tax. If you have a state income tax, determine your bracket and add the appropriate percentage. Also deduct the total of these percentages from your stated wages.

The result will give your total net income—what you will

gain by taking this extra job. To determine your real "take-home pay" per hour, divide the number of working hours into the total net income.

2. Can You Arrange a Suitable Schedule? "Time schedules are an important factor to women who wish to work part time," says Mrs. Alice K. Leopold, director of the Women's Bureau of the U. S. Department of Labor. "One woman may find that mid-day hours when the children are in school are the best time for her to work. Another may decide on an evening or week-end job, when other members of the family are free to take care of the children. Whatever the hours, it is usually necessary that they be on a regular basis, so that the employer may be assured of having the worker on the job during scheduled hours."

3. Are You Qualified for the Job You Seek? Mrs. Leopold advises: "First, assess your abilities and experience in terms of the qualifications required in the various occupations and industries which offer part-time work. You may have to convince employers not only of your abilities but also of the feasibility of a part-time schedule. In addition, you may have to compromise on the particular hours to be worked and arrangements to suit the employer's needs."

4. Will Your Family Suffer Emotionally? In his text book, "Consumer Problems and Personal Finance" (McGraw-Hill Book Co., pg. 42) Professor Arch W. Troelstrup of Stephens College cites six instances when a wife should not work but should be a home-maker on a full-time basis:

"When it is necessary for the happiness and morale of the husband.

"When the children need her. Most small children coming home from school want to be greeted by mother.

"When the wife's job forces her to tear away from the children in the morning without giving them the help and guidance necessary for cleanliness, neat dressing, and nutritious eating, and for the sense of security felt by the child who can say: 'Good-bye, Mom, see you after school.'

"When she finds that she is returning from work too tired to be civil, and before long she is snapping at husband and children.

"When she begins to feel guilty about neglecting the family and is developing the habit of lavishing too much affection on a child, of forgiving him for matters that require sensible discipline, and perhaps undermining the household assistant who cares for the child during the day.

"When the job does not permit sufficient fun and recreation with the entire family together."

Researchers of the Marriage Council of Philadelphia found that troubles generally increase when a wife works against her husband's wishes. There tend to be more quarrels about how the home is managed, about who should do what household tasks and look after the children, about how the family's income should be spent. They concluded that a wife who decides to work should make sure that her husband favors the idea, that both clearly agree how her income will be used, and what extra household tasks, if any, the husband will perform.

5. Will a Second Income Really Solve Your Problems? If you find it difficult to live within one income—especially a fairly high one—you may find it difficult to live within the second income as well. One mother took a good-paying "temporary" job to buy a second car, to outfit her two small children with expensive clothing and to provide many other luxuries. Soon the family depended upon her income as completely as upon her husband's and she found it difficult to quit. When she became pregnant and had to give all those things up, she became highly resentful—and held the baby responsible.

Leone Heuer, director of the Money Management Institute of Household Finance, says that if a husband and wife work, they should try to meet their regular expenses on his income, and to deposit hers, less expenses in connection with her job, in the family savings account. This procedure serves several purposes:

It keeps income intact for major goals like furnishing an apartment or buying a home.

Income is not dribbled away on minor purchases, nor is it used for luxuries which raise the family's living standards and tend to become habitual.

If the wife gives up her job, the couple will not have to make drastic changes in their day-to-day living expenses.

Where are the Part-Time Jobs for Women?

Mrs. Alice K. Leopold, director of the Women's Bureau of the U. S. Department of Labor, reveals that a recent survey by her Bureau turned up these common job opportunities:

TEACHERS. About 165,000 women held part-time teaching jobs outside of colleges and universities in 1958. Many were substitutes for regular teachers who were ill or unable to perform their duties. Others taught in evening schools. Many specialized in special subjects like music, arts and crafts. Some cities and towns maintain regular lists of substitutes, and a woman on a list probably will be called regularly. Qualifications for teachers vary in different states, but many require the same ones as for regular teachers.

Part-time teachers can also find college jobs. A survey by the National Educational Association shows that three out of ten of all teachers in higher institutions work part-time.

LIBRARIANS. Part-time jobs may be found in public or school libraries. Part-time professional librarians must have a year's special training after graduation from a four-year college. They often get paid about as much as full-time librarians on a per hour basis.

PROFESSIONAL NURSES. A shortage of full-time nurses enables part-time workers to get jobs easily. According to the

American Hospital Association, part-time nurses totalled two-fifths of all general duty nurses employed in hospitals in 1958. Their salaries per hour roughly equal those who work full time. There also are many openings for private duty nurses in hospitals and homes.

OTHER WORKERS IN HEALTH FIELD. Some women serve as occupational and physical therapists or as dietitians, dental hygienists, medical technologists, and x-ray technicians. Job opportunities are particularly good for part-time dental hygienists in private dental offices, and they can often work half-days or a few full days a week. Graduation from a dental hygiene school and a state license are generally required.

SOCIAL WORKERS. There is an increased need for full-time social workers with a Master's degree from an accredited school of social work.

OTHER PROFESSIONAL AND TECHNICAL WORKERS. Many employment opportunities exist for part-time artists, writers, designers, entertainers, photographers, athletes, sports instructors, and welfare and religious workers. If you have writing ability and can spend a few hours a day, you might become a local correspondent for a newspaper. Such correspondents generally provide the newspaper with stories about their neighborhood. Many self-employed writers and artists sell stories, art work, etc., to newspapers and magazines.

SECRETARIES, STENOGRAPHERS, TYPISTS. Most secretaries and stenographers are hired on a full-time basis, but many opportunities exist for part-time typists. Openings with regular hours of less than 35 hours per week are available in doctors' and dentists' offices, schools, welfare and religious services. Some firms need part-time help to meet special orders or to relieve regular employees on their time off.

Some part-time typists work in their home, during hours of their own choosing, and are paid on the basis of their actual work.

PROOFING-MACHINE OPERATORS. Banks sometimes

hire them to help balance their books after closing hours and to relieve regular employees. The machines list and sort checks and can be operated with relatively little instruction. Many operators work four to five hours each afternoon and their hourly earnings are sometimes higher than those of full-time employees.

CASHIERS. One survey revealed that almost one-fifth of all cashiers in stores, movie theaters, etc. were part-time employees. Many opportunities exist as grocery checkers in large food chains, where two-thirds of the cashiers may work part-time. A typical work schedule includes two evenings a week—probably Thursday and Friday—and all day Saturday.

TELEPHONE OPERATORS. Telephone companies, hotels and other enterprises which keep switchboards open around-the-clock use part-time operators.

OTHER CLERICAL WORKERS. Many firms need book-keepers, office-machine operators, receptionists, file clerks, library assistants, telephone ad-takers, or survey enumerators. Research firms which seek to learn what consumers think about various products will hire researchers to question people in their homes.

SALES PERSONS. Sales work is a major source of employment. More than a million women earn part-time incomes in general merchandise and clothing stores, etc. Generally no special knowledge is required, and the work is often done evenings and Saturdays.

Sales jobs in department stores often are ideal for mothers of school children. These stores generally open about 9:30 A.M., so mothers can send their youngsters to school before they go to work and can often return home before school is dismissed.

Many firms also hire women as door-to-door and telephone sales agents. Some insurance companies hire women and allow them to decide the hours they will work. However, extensive training in insurance principles is required. In two-thirds of the states, agents must pass a written examination before they can sell.

Part-time positions as real estate agents are also open, but extensive training is necessary.

WAITRESSES. Eating and drinking places traditionally use part-time waitresses for their various meal periods. Waitresses sometimes receive higher hourly wages than full-time workers, and tips also add to their earnings.

HOSTESSES. They supervise waiters and waitresses, and usually must have an attractive appearance and pleasant personality. They generally work a few hours daily during meal periods.

BEAUTY OPERATORS. Part-time jobs are available in many shops due to marked weekly fluctuation in demand for beauty services. Since beauty shops are often located in local shopping centers, a beauty operator may find a suitable opening in her own neighborhood. Wages may be on a commission basis or straight hourly rate, with tips extra. A state license is usually required.

PRACTICAL NURSES. Part-time jobs are numerous in hospitals and private homes. All states (but not the District of Columbia) require practical nurses to be licensed, and a year's training period is generally required before one can take the examination.

CHARWOMEN and CLEANERS. Little or no experience or training is required. Cleaning workers generally work during evening hours in offices and stores after the close of the business day. Some women work as maids in hotels for one or two days per week.

OTHER SERVICE WORKERS. Some elevator operators work part-time in department stores and office buildings. Previous experience is not usually required, since it takes only a short time to learn to operate modern automatic elevators.

A small number of women are in "protective service" occupations—patrolling school crossings, checking parking meters. Some work as ushers in theaters, etc., usually on evenings and week-ends.

PRIVATE HOUSEHOLD WORKERS. They represent the largest single occupation group of part-time workers. Almost 2,000,000 worked part time during 1958—as domestic servants, baby-sitters, home laundresses, housekeepers, cooks, governesses. The Department of Labor says private household work offers the largest number of part-time employment opportunities for non-white women. Hours, arrangements and earnings are extremely varied.

OPERATIVES. Over 600,000 women worked part time in this category during 1958—about 16 percent of all women working as operatives. Many were employed in manufacturing, or as dressmakers and seamstresses, bus and taxi drivers, and laundry and dry-cleaning operatives.

FARM WORKERS. Almost two million women work part time on farms, but about two-thirds are unpaid family members working as farm laborers.

How Can You Go About Getting a Part-Time Job?

Mrs. Leopold states that employers in the service and trade industries use public and private employment agencies, newspaper advertisements and word-of-mouth. In one city, restaurants have their own employment agency to fill jobs for waitresses, cashiers, hostesses and kitchen help. Hotels in another city cooperate with the unions in running an agency.

Department and specialty stores often use ads to recruit part-time sales persons, but many persons obtain jobs by applying directly to the stores. Food stores also use advertising and public employment services to find part-time workers. Some chain stores with several outlets in a city have a central hiring office. Food stores often post signs listing job openings in their windows.

Most charwomen and cleaners in buildings are hired through unions or by the employer upon direct application. A person seeking work in a private household is likely to get it by asking friends doing this work if they know of any openings, by applying to public and private employment agencies, or by answering newspaper ads.

Professional workers often use placement services in their professional associations. Where jobs are easy to obtain, such as nursing and social work, they generally apply directly to the particular institutions or social agencies where they would like to work.

Women seeking part-time work as school teachers apply directly to local Boards of Education. Most school systems maintain a register of persons available for substitute work.

Clerical workers can often find positions through employment agencies, advertisement, and personal contacts. Some find fairly regular part-time work by accepting a job with an agency which places them in different firms requesting temporary help. The agencies then place them on their payrolls and seek the jobs for them. In addition, business schools sometimes operate placement services for their graduates.

Before You Start Your Own Business

Many young couples regard a business of their own as the solution to their financial problems—the key to their future financial security.

Here are the questions they often ask about operating a business—with the answers by Hilton Davis, Manager of the Domestic Distribution Department of the United States Chamber of Commerce:

Is it generally easy to operate your own business? "No, it is more complex and difficult than most people realize. You'll have to work hard and long to make a go of it. But the rewards are worth it. You'll be the head man. Nobody can fire you.

Your opportunity for income will be greater. You'll have more pride in your own abilities. And you'll experience a satisfaction that words can't describe."

What chance would your business have to survive? "Since World War II, a new firm has had a 50-50 chance of lasting two years under the same management. Chances are three to one against its living four years. Only one out of five businesses lasts ten years."

What are the causes of failure? "The actual reasons, based on research by Dun & Bradstreet in the retail field in 1958, were inexperience and incompetence, 91.8%; neglect, 3.6%; fraud, 1.8%; disaster, 1.5%; reason unknown, 1.3%. Chances are that a substantial portion of those that failed would have succeeded if they had just prepared themselves adequately."

What kind of people make good owners and managers of their own store? "Authorities say they rate high in most of these character traits:

"*Initiative:* They are self-starters; don't wait for directions.

"*Positiveness:* They are optimistic, self-confident, willing to take risks.

"*Leadership:* They are forceful, inspire confidence and loyalty.

"*Responsibility:* They accept it—don't duck it.

"*Organizing ability:* They can see what should be done and get it done in a logical order.

"*Industriousness:* They are willing, capable of working hard for long hours.

"*Decisiveness:* They are quick and accurate, not hesitant.

"*Sincerity:* They are square-shooters, on the level, honest.

"*Perseverance:* They have stick-to-it-iveness, particularly when hours are long and business seems slow.

"*Physical Energy:* They are highly energetic at all times.

"*Friendliness:* They have the ability to get along with people, even those who try one's patience."

What type of business is best for you? "Nobody can answer

that but you yourself. But experience in a particular kind of business is especially useful. If you have worked in a shoe store, you will already have some of the knowledge you need to run one and will be better-equipped to do it well. The more experience and training you have in operating a particular business, the more likely your success.

"Until you've gotten some experience in a business, it's hard to know whether you could do well in it. So get experience working for somebody else before you try it yourself. This way, you actually get steady pay until you are ready for the big plunge of your own."

What kind of business may be needed in your area? "Best way to find out is to ask questions of people who live in the area, wholesalers who service the area, the local chamber of commerce, local businessmen. Ask enough people and you'll get a pretty good idea of what's needed."

Is location important? "Depending on the type of business, you must be sure there are enough people in your shopping area to support your store. The right location sometimes saves a poorly-run business; the wrong location can wreck an otherwise superbly-managed store."

How do you start? "If you buy an existing business, you can inherit your predecessor's good will and customers. He may leave experienced employees who will be either a great help or resentful of new ownership, depending on how you handle them. You will have to decide how much you should pay for the business, whether it is going up or has been going downhill, and whether you can get rent, credit, etc. on as favorable terms as your predecessor.

"If you start a new business, you have several advantages—and handicaps. You make your own good will and are not saddled with hung-over ill-will from a previous operator. But everything will have to be done from scratch. You may even need more capital since it will take months—perhaps years—before you can build a substantial customer-following.

"Leasing or renting a business is often done—for example, with gas stations. You take less of the risk, but must pay something extra to the lessor for assuming part of your risk. Negotiation of the contract is very important. Unless it is advantageous to both you and the firm you make it with, there will be difficulties.

"A lot of people spend all their money to get their doors open and then do not have the reserve necessary to keep them in business for the year or two necessary to build up a following."

What You Must Know to Run a Business

How much is involved in operating a business? "You might divide up the work of running a store like this:

• *"Controls or record-keeping:* This includes accounting, inventories, estimating financial conditions—and pricing your goods or services so that mark-ups will cover your expenses, plus some profit, and still be low enough to be competitive and attract customers.

• *"Selling, Promotion, Merchandising, Advertising, Display:* Those activities which move the goods toward the customer, the customer toward the store, at the right time and place—and make the sales. You can't be passive about this part if you want to do business.

• *"Buying:* You'll have to know where to buy your stock or equipment—what to pay for it—how to determine quality of goods—how much to buy—how to arrange appropriate credit terms and promotional support from suppliers.

• *"Handling employees:* You'll have to select and train them—and keep their morale high. They reflect your attitude, and the success of the store is involved.

• *"Planning ahead:* Many operators get involved in doing the next thing and neglect the long-and-short range planning which pays big dividends.

• *"Developing a business personality:* Try to give your business an identity that makes it different from other stores. Decide what your customers expect from you—then stress that quality.

• *"Community participation:* Participation in your chamber of commerce and in your local political processes is the way you help shape the future of your town, your state and your country.

• *"Taxes, auditing, finance and insurance:* You will probably need professional advice and counsel."

Should you make your business a partnership? "If so, be careful to choose a partner experienced in parts of the business where you are weak. Suppose you are skilled in accounting, inventories, record-keeping and financial management. You might seek a partner with experience in selling and buying. Together, you might make a fine team."

Are You the Type to Run Your Own Business?

The Small Business Administration says that the first question you should answer after recognizing that there is a dark side as well as a bright side to the prospect of establishing your own business is "Am I the type?" It is important that you appraise your strong points and weak points.

Below is a list of 10 important traits for the person operating his own business. Add others that you think are significant for the type of business you desire to establish. Then rate yourself realistically and ask a few friends to rate you.

Are most of your check marks on the left-hand side of the page? They should be. But perhaps you can compensate for your weak points by hiring the right help or obtaining associates whose strong points offset your weak ones. If you are weak in too many traits, do not undertake the venture.

Initiative Additional tasks sought; highly ingenious	Resourceful; alert to opportunities	Regular work performed without waiting for directions	Routine worker awaiting directions
Attitude toward others Positive; friendly interest in people	Pleasant, polite	Sometimes difficult to work with	Inclined to be quarrelsome or uncooperative
Leadership Forceful, inspiring confidence and loyalty	Order giver	Driver	Weak
Responsibility Responsibility sought and welcomed	Accepted without protest	Unwilling to assume without protest	Avoided whenever possible
Organizing ability Highly capable of perceiving and arranging fundamentals in logical order	Able organizer	Fairly capable of organizing	Poor organizer
Industry Industrious; capable of working hard for long hours	Can work hard, but not for too long a period	Fairly industrious	Hard work avoided
Decision Quick and accurate	Good and careful	Quick, but often unsound	Hesitant and fearful
Sincerity Courageous, square-shooter	On the level	Fairly	Inclined to lack sincerity
Perseverance Highly steadfast in purpose; not discouraged by obstacles	Effort steadily maintained	Average determination and persistence	Little or no persistence
Physical energy Highly energetic at all times	Energetic most of time	Fairly energetic	Below average

—Source: Small Business Administration

Directions:

Place a check mark on the line following each trait where you think it ought to be. The check mark need not be placed directly over one of the guide phrases, because the rating may lie somewhere between the phrases.

chapter twelve

YOU ARE PREPARING FOR RETIREMENT

Your Social Security payments provide the base to give you peace of mind in your old age

A 33-year-old man recently asked his banker when he should begin to plan for his retirement. He said that he had been employed steadily since he took his first job at the age of 19.

"Then you began planning 14 years ago," the banker said. "And you have the best foundation to build on."

The banker was referring, of course, to Social Security—the federal system of insurance which came into being in 1936 and which provides for monthly payments for most men reaching 65, women reaching 62, and others—such as widows with dependent children—regardless of their age.

Social Security combines life insurance upon the life of the bread-winner and head of a family and old-age insurance. It is operated by the Federal Government out of taxes paid in by employees and employers and self-employed individuals. Like any other kind of insurance, how much Social Security money is paid out to you in your old age—or to a widow or dependent children in case the father dies—depends upon the amount paid in. And the amount paid in depends, in turn, upon the amount of your earnings and how long you have worked in employment or self-employment covered by Social Security.

You Are Preparing for Retirement

How much work is required in order for you to be "insured" when you reach retirement age depends on when you were born. A person who reaches retirement age in 1961 will need credit for 3¼ years of work under Social Security. One reaching retirement age in 1971 or later will need 10 years.

The amount you will receive in retirement is figured from your average earnings in covered employment and self-employment up to the year you become entitled to benefits—at retirement age or later. The more regularly you work under Social Security and the higher your earnings, the higher your benefit will be.

• *The Meaning of "Retired."* You need not stop working entirely to be "retired" under the law. If you earn up to $1,200 a year, you can get all your Social Security payments for that year. If you earn over $1,200, you will have $1 of your Social Security payments withheld for each dollar that you earn from $1,200 to $1,500. For every $1 that you earn above $1,500, $1 of your payments (or your family payments) will be withheld. However, you can still get payments for any month you neither work for more than $100 nor render substantial services in self-employment. At no time is any income you get from insurance or investments counted as earnings. You may receive payments when you are age 72 or older no matter how much you earn.

• *Family Benefits When You Retire.* When you receive old-age benefits, payments can also be made to certain dependents. Among them: your unmarried children under 18; a disabled child 18 or older (if the disability began before age 18); your wife, if she is caring for a child receiving payments; your wife, 62 or older; or your dependent husband 65 or over.

You will be fully insured on reaching retirement age if you have the number of quarters of coverage shown in the table below. If you lack enough quarters of coverage when you reach retirement age, you may earn them after that time.

Quarters of Coverage Needed

Year in which you were born		Year in which you reach retirement age	
Men	Women		
1896	1899	1961	13
1897	1900	1962	14
1898	1901	1963	16
1899	1902	1964	17
1900	1903	1965	18
1901	1904	1966	20
1902	1905	1967	21
1903	1906	1968	22
1904	1907	1969	24
1905	1908	1970	25
1906	1909	1971	26
1907	1910	1972	28
1908	1911	1973	29
1909	1912	1974	30
1910	1913	1975	32
1911	1914	1976	33
1912	1915	1977	34
1913	1916	1978	36
1914	1917	1979	37
1915	1918	1980	38
1916 or later	1919 or later	1981 or later	40

—Source: Social Security Administration, Nov., 1960

• *Social Security Taxes.* Federal old-age benefits are paid for by a tax based on the worker's earnings. If you are employed, you and your employer share the tax equally. If you are self-employed, you pay all the tax, but at a lower rate than the combined rate for an employee and his employer.

If you are employed, your tax is deducted from your wages each payday. Your employer sends it with his share of the tax to the District Director of Internal Revenue. If you are self-employed and earn $400 or more in a year, you pay your tax when you file your individual income tax return. You must pay this tax even if you are not required to pay any income tax.

You Are Preparing for Retirement 201

This table shows tax rates by years:

Calendar Year	Employee	Employer	Self-Employed
1960-62	3%	3%	4½%
1963-65	3½%	3½%	5¼%
1966-68	4%	4%	6%
1969 and over	4½%	4½%	6¾%

• *What you should know about Social Security now.* Presumably it will be many years before you apply for retirement benefits. Quite likely, the laws covering the payments you will get will have changed considerably by that time. You probably need not concern yourself now with the exact figures involved.

It is important, however, that you understand how to make sure that you will be eligible for benefits when retirement time comes.

If your work is covered by the Social Security Act, you must have a Social Security account number. This number, which is shown on your Social Security card, is used to keep a record of your earnings. You should use the same number all your life to avoid getting your account confused with one or more of the 179 million names in the Social Security records, some of which may be exactly like yours.

When you take a job, show your card to your employer so that he may use your name and account number exactly as they appear on the card when he reports your wages. If you are self-employed, copy your name and account number on the form you use to report your net earnings for Social Security credit.

The nearest Social Security office will issue a new card or a duplicate to replace a lost card. If your town has no Social Security office, get an application blank at the post office. If you change your name, get a new card with the old account number but your new name.

The law requires each employer to give you receipts for your Social Security taxes he has deducted. At the end of each year he must give you a form (W-2) which will show the exact amount taken from your pay. You should keep records of self-employment income you have reported.

You may check your official Social Security credits by asking the Social Security Administration, Baltimore 35, Md., for a statement of your account. Local Social Security offices have addressed postcards you can use in requesting this information. You should make this check at least once each 3 years, since corrections can be made only within a limited period.

District offices of the Social Security Administration are conveniently located throughout the country, and representatives travel regularly to other communities. They will answer any of your questions about any provisions of Social Security.

But Social Security Can't Do It All

If you work consistently from your twenties until you reach retirement age, you will have a good cushion in Social Security payments you will get. They will enable you to avoid dire poverty, but will not permit you to afford ordinary comforts and luxuries you have become accustomed to. During your earning years, you will have to do some additional saving on your own.

Some 3,000 Americans reach 65 each day. Of these:

Only one person in 24 has an income of $5,000 or more.

Only one in eight receives over $3,000 a year.

Less than one in four has an annual income of $2,000 or more.

Those statistics prove why you yourself must take extra steps to insure your successful retirement. You should:

Set a goal for your retirement financial needs.

Provide for unexpected contingencies—prolonged illness, untimely death, etc.—with a cash reserve in liquid savings and life insurance.

Set aside as much money as you will need to assure you that your retirement objectives will be met.

You Can "Buy a Steady Income" for Your Declining Years

Most people nourish the great hope that they will have a steady monthly income they can live on from the time they retire until they die. This hope can be realized in part through Social Security, part through savings accounts, and part through a pension or annuity.

Here is what you should know about annuities. It is based upon a report by R. Wilfred Kelsey and Arthur C. Daniels, officials of the Institute of Life Insurance.

A LIFE ANNUITY will pay an income for the remaining lifetime of the contract owner (the annuitant). People buy life annuities because they want a steady income in old age if they outlive their earning period. Life insurance policies and annuity contracts often complement each other, because proceeds of policies may provide an annuity income—while some types of annuities include insurance protection.

AN INDIVIDUAL ANNUITY will provide an income for yourself, generally (but not necessarily) in your old age. You pay premiums directly to the company in one payment or in regular installments. You can get annuity contracts that will pay you so many units of $10 monthly income or $100 annual income starting at a specific age. They are also issued in terms of income purchased at say age 65 by $100 of annual premiums or $1,000 of single premium.

A GROUP ANNUITY (OR PENSION) is generally taken out by an employer for his employees under a master contract. The employer generally pays part of the cost and employees' shares are deducted from their wages. There are two main types of Group Annuity Plans.

Under the Unit Benefit Plan, you get a "paid-up unit of

benefit" at 65 for each year you work in the firm. This "unit of benefit" may run from one to two percent of your earnings for the year. Suppose you work 30 years under a 1½ percent benefit plan and you earn an average of $8,000 per year all that time. You would receive an annual retirement income of 45% (30 times 1½%) of your average wages. This would amount to $3,600 a year or $300 a month.

Under the Money Purchase Plan, a fixed percentage of your salary will be used to buy "paid-up units of income." Your employer also contributes a certain amount—perhaps the same as your contribution, perhaps a proportion of it.

Group Annuity Plans provide death benefits at least equal to the employee's contributions. You can withdraw the amount of your contributions if you leave your job, or you can leave them and get the benefits at retirement age purchased by your contributions. Most plans also provide that when you reach a certain age or work for a certain number of years, or both, you are also entitled to the benefits at retirement age paid for by your employer, even if you change jobs thereafter. But you are not allowed to cash them in.

ANNUITIES IN INSURANCE POLICIES. Annuities are often included as an income provision of ordinary life insurance policies. The insured may specify an annuity type settlement instead of a lump sum settlement for his beneficiary or the beneficiary can do this. Some policies permit the insured himself to take the cash value of his policy in the form of income at a certain age.

A "straight life" annuity will pay you an income during your remaining lifetime, but all payments cease upon your death. This type of annuity furnishes the largest amount of lifetime income per dollar of purchase money and is recommended for the person who wants maximum income for himself. However, some people dislike the idea of "losing"—of receiving less in income than they have paid in. Actually, they have the chance of receiving a great deal more than they pay in. For the excess funds that come about from those annuitants who die early go to those who live a long time and receive more than their purchase money.

A "guaranteed" annuity will pay you an income for life. But if you die within the guarantee period, income payments for the balance of this period will go to a beneficiary you select. This period is usually 10 to 20 years. The company is obligated to pay income benefits, in any case, for the 10 or 20 years.

An "installment refund" annuity will pay you an income for life. But if you die before you receive as much money as you have paid, income payments will be continued to your beneficiary until total payments equal that amount.

A "cash refund" annuity will also pay you an income for life. If you die before you receive as much as you paid, the balance will go in a lump sum to your beneficiary.

IMMEDIATE AND DEFERRED ANNUITIES. You can buy an annuity contract to provide an income beginning either immediately or years later on a date you choose. You can also decide whether you want the income to be paid monthly, quarterly, semi-annually or annually.

Immediate annuities are generally purchased by people in middle or later life. Here is a typical example. When George Block retired as a reporter for a large press association, he and his wife had managed to save some money, but it would not earn enough income for them to live on, even when added to their Social Security benefits. They decided to buy an immediate annuity of the joint survivor type. In this way, they could dig into their savings for living expenses and could be sure that they would never be in want.

Deferred annuities provide for an income to begin some time later. While you can buy this annuity with a single premium, most are paid for over a period of years. Deferred annuities are usually bought by people who do not need or who already have adequate life insurance protection. Most deferred annuity plans are actually savings plans which build up a fund which buys an immediate annuity at the end of the deferred period. Here are two examples:

A "retirement income" annuity may meet your needs if you want to save regularly for a life income and need no insurance protection. This contract is really an accumulation at interest of premiums paid, less expenses.

Brenda Adams is a secretary. She saves regularly, has sizeable "rainy day" savings and a life insurance policy that would pay her burial expenses. She has been advised to buy a "retirement income" annuity for her retirement. Her beneficiary—a sister—will receive at least all the premiums she has paid in. Miss Adams will have a fund to borrow on in case of need. And she can cash in the policy whenever she wishes. Except for the early years she will receive at least what she paid in.

A "retirement income" policy includes a substantial insurance element. Otherwise it is identical to the "retirement income" annuity.

This policy is often suggested to single people, because they get all the insurance protection they need while most of their premium dollars build up for their retirement benefits. People with dependents who have enough insurance also find this policy helpful, because it lays principal stress on building a retirement income. For instance, James and Christine Logan have two children, their own home, a substantial savings account, and enough life insurance to cover a college education for each child. They do not want to be a burden on anyone in their old age, so they took out a Retirement Income Policy consisting of $20,000 insurance on James' life. It also provides for an income of $200.00 a month when he becomes 65.

JOINT LIFE AND SURVIVORSHIP ANNUITIES. Most annuities are based on the life of one person. However, you can buy an annuity covering two or more persons which will pay an income until the second or last person dies. Say you and your spouse take out such an annuity. You can get a plan which continues the full amount until the second person dies. Another plan provides that if one person dies, the second will receive two-thirds or one-half of the original income. This plan operates on the fact that living expenses of one person are lower than for two. Most joint life and survivorship annuities are immediate annuities, purchased in middle or later life.

These annuities are becoming popular for setting the proceeds of ordinary life policies. They are often chosen instead of single life annuities payable under Group Annuity plans.

"ANTI-INFLATION" ANNUITIES. Some life insurance companies have sought legal permission to sell a "variable annuity"—one designed to protect savings against loss of purchasing power from inflation.

A buyer would pay a fixed premium for 15 years or longer. His premiums would be invested mainly in common stock, but might also be in preferred stock or convertible bonds. The value of his total investment would vary with the level of the stock market and with fluctuations in dividend rates, and the income he would receive would depend largely upon this value at the time the annuity payment fell due.

Sometimes conditions change and a person who has not yet begun to receive income payments under his annuity wishes to change his retirement age—to retire, say, at 60 instead of 65 as he had planned. This can be arranged with the insurance company, often as a matter of contract right. The company will then have to make payments for a longer period of time and therefore each payment will be smaller.

Or suppose you had expected to retire at 65 but want to continue working when you reach that age. You can arrange to forego annuity payments while you are working, but you may be permitted to continue your contributions. In this way you will receive higher benefits when you finally retire.

A Savings Schedule for Retirement

How much would you like to have when you retire at age 65? This table shows how much you must save each year for each $1,000 you hope to have then. The figures are based on the assumption that you will place your savings in a savings institution with interest compounded annually and will let all dividends or interest accumulate.

Your Age Now	Interest Rate		
	3%	4%	7%
50	$54.00	$50.00	$40.00
45	37.00	33.50	24.50
40	27.50	24.00	16.00
35	21.00	18.00	10.50
30	16.50	13.50	7.00

Three Questions to Answer Before You Buy an Annuity

Insurance experts say that you should exercise the same cautions in buying annuities as you would in buying a policy on your life. You should also have these points clarified:

• *How will you pay for the annuity?* You can buy one with a single premium, or with premiums spread out over a long period. If you buy one on an installment basis, make sure that you will be able to keep up the payments without difficulty.

• *How will annuity payments be made?* As described above, there are many variations in the way you can be paid off and in what will happen to unused monies after you die. If a survivor must be protected—for example, your spouse—make sure that the annuity will carry on after your death as in the Joint and Survivor Annuity, or has a guaranteed period of income that would provide for her adequately.

• *Is the insurance company reliable?* It is important to investigate it thoroughly. You want to make sure that it will be in business and able to make the annuity payments when you retire. Your whole future depends upon it.

About the Author

John L. Springer's byline is a familiar one to millions of readers of America's top magazines. He was for many years a feature writer for the Associated Press, specializing in articles on home ownership, taxes, and money management. He has written more than a hundred articles on these subjects for national magazines, and has travelled from coast to coast to gather material exposing rackets which prey upon American consumers. He has drawn upon his wide contacts among experts in all parts of the country to bring you the up-to-date information contained in this book. He is a graduate of St. John's and New York Universities, and lives with his wife and three children in Scarsdale, New York.

INDEX

A

Adams, Brenda, 206
advertisements, interpretation of, 19, 20
AFL-CIO, *see* American Federation of Labor-Congress of Industrial Organizations
Allied Home Owners' Association of Roslyn, Long Island, 151
Allison, Frank O., vi
American Bankers Association, v, 9, 113
American Express Co., 52
American Federation of Labor-Congress of Industrial Organizations, 38
American Hospital Association, 187
American Institute of Architects, 157
American Institute of Family Relations, vii, xii
American Medical Association, 103, 107
American Stock Exchange, 126, 133, 139
annuity,
  anti-inflation, 207
  deferred, 205, 206
  immediate, 205
  life, 203
Arizona, 175
Associated Press, 209
Association of Better Business Bureau, Inc., v, 13, 19, 20, 61, 91, 107
Association of Mutual Banks, 59
Association of Stock Exchange Firms, 139
automobile,
  expenses of, 6, 7
  financing costs of, 49, 50
  insurance, 95ff

B

bait advertising, 31
Baltimore, Md., 202
Baltimore Better Business Bureau, 174
Bank money order, 117
Barron's, 127
Bateman, J. Carrol, vi, 95
beef, grades of, 25
Bernhard, Charles H., vi
Better Business Bureau, 28, 29, 33, 108, 165
"blind merchandise," 16
Block, George, 205
Block, Lee F., v
Blount, Gerald R., 27
Blue Cross Association, v, 103, 104
bonds, 123
"book value," discussed, 128
Boston, 30
Boston Better Business Bureau, 48
Brandeis, Louis, 89
Brown, Ann, 125
building and loan association, *see* savings and loan association
Bureau of Old Age and Survivors Insurance, v, 75
Business Week, 127

C

Cadillac, 99
calf, grades of, 26
California, xv
Canada, 29, 122
car, *see* automobile
Casady, Clyde S., vi, 89
Castro, Fidel, 129
Central Credit Bureau, 39
Central Credit Exchange, 39

Chamber of Commerce of the United States, v
charge account, discussed, 42
charge account, regular, 42
check,
  cashiers, 117
  certified, 117
  endorsement of, 118
  processing of, 116
checkbook, use and balancing of, 115, 118
checking account,
  discussed, 113ff
  joint, 113
  regular, 114
  special, 114
Chesseldean, Raymond, v
Chevrolet, 99
Chicago, 72
Chicago Better Business Bureau, 30
Christgau, Victor, v, 75
Clarke, Charles C., vi
closed-end company, discussed, 135
closing costs, 155, 156
C.L.U., vi
Cofer, Eloise, v
collateral loans, discussed, 46
collision, 97
commercial banks, 66
common stock, 122
comparison shopping, 15
comprehensive insurance, 97
Connecticut, 65, 90
Consumer Department of the AFL-CIO, 38
consumer finance company loans, 46
Consumer Problems and Personal Finance, vii, 42
contracts, discussed, 30
conventional bank loans, 46
conventional life insurance company, 87
convertible debentures, 123
convertible preferred stock, 123
cooperative bank, *see* savings and loan association
Cooperative League of the U.S.A., vi, 47
Cranwill, Alfred, vi
credit,
  as a convenience, 36
  as a tax help, 37
  costs of, 48
  discussed, 34ff

credit (*Cont.*):
  how to buy on, 41
  revolving, 43
Credit Bureau of Greater New York, v, 40
credit cards, 52
credit union, 47, 67
Credit Union National Association, vi, 44, 53
Crenson, Charlotte, v
Cuba, 129

D

Dakins, J. Gordon, vi
Dallas, Texas, 39, 74
Daniels, Arthur C., vi, 203
Dauer, Dr. Ernst A., vi
Davis, Hilton, v, 191
Deindorfer, Robert G., vi
Department of Agriculture, 183
Detroit, 57
development house, 167
Dime Savings Bank of Brooklyn, vi, 175
Diner's Club, 52
disability income, 84
disability waiver of premium, 84
District of Columbia, 189
doctor's bill insurance, 104
Domestic Distribution Department of the Chamber of Commerce of the United States, v, 191
double indemnity, 84
Dow Jones Industrial Average, 136
Dun and Bradstreet, 192
dwelling insurance, 99, 100

E

"E" bonds, *see* U.S. Government "E" bonds
Eberly, Marion Stevens, vi, xv, 6
Eisinger, Larry, vi, 169, 170, 171
endowment insurance, 82, 83
extended payment plan, 42

F

The Family in a Money World, vii, xvii
family protection coverage, 97
Family Service Association of America, vi, vii, xvii

Index

Fawcett Books, vi, 169
FDIC, see Federal Deposit Insurance Corporation
Federal Deposit Insurance Corporation, 59, 61, 64, 65, 66
Federal Home Loan Bank, 64
Federal Home Loan Bank Board, 144
Federal Home Loan Bank System, 59
Federal Housing Administration, 146, 147, 148, 149, 150, 153
Federal Reserve Bank of New York, vi
Federal Reserve Board, 59
Federal Savings and Loan Insurance Corporation, 61, 64
Federal Trade Commission, v, 32
Feldman, Professor Frances Lomas, vii, xvii
Fichtel, Rudolph R., v
Financial World, 127
Florida, 175
food, discussed, 3ff
Forbes, 127, 135, 137
Franklin, Ben, 58
Frese, Robert C., vi, 175
fruit, grades and types of, 27, 28
FSLIC, see Federal Savings and Loan Insurance Corporation

G

G.I. insurance, see National Service Life Insurance
Great Lakes, xv
group dental care, 111
Group Health Association, Inc., of Washington, D.C., vi, 109, 110, 111
group insurance, 86
guarantees, limitations and terms of, 31

H

"H" bonds, see U.S. Government "H" bonds
Hamilton, Anne, xiii
Health Insurance Institute, vi, 5
Heuer, Leone Anne, vi, 6, 7, 185
home and personal property insurance, 99
"homeowners," policy, 99
homestead association, see savings and loan association

hospital and health insurance, 103
Household Finance Corporation, vi, 2, 50, 185
How to Build and Contract Your Own Home, 169
How to Live 365 Days a Year, vii, xiii

I

impulse spending, 14
installment payment plan, 43
Institute of Home Economics, U.S. Department of Agriculture, 3, 23, 26
Institute of Life Insurance, vi, 6, 79, 85, 91, 107
insurance,
 auto, 95
 comprehensive, 97
 cost of, 91
 doctor's bill, 104
 double indemnity, 84
 dwelling, 99
 endowment, 82
 family plan, 83
 family protection coverage, 97
 group, 86
 home & personal property, 96
 "homeowners policy," 99
 hospital and health, 103
 liability, 96
 loss-of-income, 105
 major medical expenses, 104
 medical payment, 97
 ordinary life, 82
 personal liability, 101
 personal property, 100
 term, 81
 title, 102
Insurance Information Institute, vi, 96, 99, 101
insurance loans, discussed, 45
Internal Revenue, 200
Investment Bankers Association of America, 139
Irwin, A. A., 24

J

Jamaica, New York, vii, 157
Johnston, Aubra, 30

K

Kelsey, R. Wilfred, vi, 203
Klein, Bill, 125

L

lamb, grades of, 25
Lawrence, Ruddick C., vi
Leopold, Alice K., v, 184, 190
liability insurance, 96
life insurance, discussed, 4, 74ff
"loan sharks," 47
Logan, James, 206
Long Island, 173
Loomis, Dave, 78
Los Angeles, vii, xii, 158
loss-of-income insurance, 105
lot, how to buy, 173
lot, mail order, 175
Lumber Retailers' Association, 171
Lutey, Warren P., v

M

McGraw-Hill Book Company, Inc., vii, 42
McKay, Al, 78
Macmillan Company, vii
Macy's, 36
Magazine of Wall Street, 127
major medical expense insurance, 104
Marriage Council of Philadelphia, 185
Marriage Is What You Make It, vii, xii
Martin, Betty S., vi
Massachusetts, 65, 96
Massachusetts Indemnity and Life Insurance Company, vi
maternity, costs of, 5
meats, discussed, 24-26
medical care and insurance, 5
medical payments insurance, 97
mobile home, *see* trailer home
Mobile Home Manufacturer's Association, 179
money
  as a tool, xi
  family conference on, xiv
  how to borrow, 45
  six principles of, xii ff
  six ways to help you manage, xii ff
Money Management Institute of the Household Finance Corporation, vi, 2, 50, 185

Money Purchase Plan, 204
Monthly Investment Plan, 137, 138
Moody's, 126, 127
Mooney, George A., vi, 134
moonlighting, discussed, 181
Mortgages, discussed, 143ff
Murray, Janet, v
mutton, grades of, 25
mutual funds, discussed, 132
mutual savings banks, discussed, 65
Mutual Savings Central Fund of Massachusetts, 65
National Association of Home Builders, 157
National Association of Investment Companies, vi, 134, 137
National Association of Real Estate Boards, vi
National Association of Security Dealers, Inc., 126, 139
National Better Business Bureau, The, 16, 178
National Education Association, 186
National Retail Merchants Association, vi
national service life insurance, 86
National Thrift Committee, 57, 72
New England, 34
New Jersey, 161
New York, xv, 47, 65, 90, 96, 169
New York City Better Business Bureau, 139
New York Stock Exchange, vi, 122, 126, 130, 133, 135, 137, 139
New York University, 209
North Carolina, 96
Nyborg, Victor H., v, 19, 61, 91

O

O'Connell, William B., vii
"odd lots," 131
Ohio, 158
Ohio State University, vi, 2
Operation, Inc., of New York, 24
options, chart of, 85
options, settlement, 84
ordinary life insurance, discussed, 82, 83
over the counter, discussed, 133

P

Parrish, Robert M., v, 32
participating preferred stock, 123

Index

Pembroke, Arthur, 126
personal liability insurance, 101, 102
personal property insurance, 100
Peters, Richard A., vi, 4
Popenoe, Dr., Paul, vii, xii
Portland, Maine, 39
Powell, Frank, 78
prefabricated houses, 169
preferred stock, 123
Prentice-Hall, Inc., vii

R

retired, meaning of, 199
retirement, discussed, 198ff
Retirement Income Policy, 206
revolving credit, discussed, 43
rights, 124
Roberts, Thomas C., v
Rosapepe, Joseph S., vi
Roslyn, Long Island, 151
"round lots," 131

S

St. John's University, 209
Sales Management Magazine, 23
Sanforized, 22
San Francisco, 57
savings, discussed, 5
savings and loan associations, discussed, 63
Savings Bank Association of Massachusetts, vi, 89
savings bank life insurance, discussed, 89
Savings Bank Life Insurance Council, vii
Savings Bank Life Insurance Council of Massachusetts, 4
savings loans, discussed, 45
Scarsdale, New York, vii, 209
Schindler, Dr. John A., vii, xiii
Sealy, Dick, 125
Secretary of Labor, v
Seelig, R. A., vii, 27
Seiter, John H., vii, 142, 153
settlement options, 84
Severa, Rudolph M., v, 40, 51
shelter, discussed, 2
shopping, fundamental rules of, 13
Small, Kenneth E., vi
Small Business Administration, 195, 196

Social Security, 55, 75, 182, 183, 198
 benefits, 77
 discussed, 75-77
Social Security Administration, v, 200, 202
special sales, 17
spending plan, 8
Spray, Mabel, vi, 2
Springer, Ellen Albright, vii
Springer, John L., 209
Standards and Poor's, 126, 127
Staten Island, New York, 169
Stephans Council, 42
Stock Market, description of workings of, 129-132
stop-loss order, 132
Stowe, S. F., v
straight life insurance, *see* ordinary life insurance
Strunk, Norman, vii, xiii, 55, 69
Sullivan, Daniel J., vi
Supermarket Institute, The, 23, 24
supermarket shopping, 22-24

T

Talmadge, Ben, 79
Taylor, Alfred, vi
"Ten Commandments" for borrowers, 53
term insurance, 81
title insurance, 102
tract house, *see* development house
trailer home, 179
Troelstrup, A. W., vii, 42, 43

U

Unit Benefit Plan, 203, 204
United Fresh Fruit and Vegetable Association, vii, 27
United States Chamber of Commerce, 191
U.S. Dept. of Agriculture, v, 3, 24, 26, 27
U.S. Dept. of Labor, 181
U.S. Government "E" Bonds, 68, 69
U.S. Government "H" Bonds, 68, 69
U.S. Pharmacopoeia, 21
U.S. Savings and Loan League, vii, xii, 55, 69, 147
U.S. Supreme Court, 89
University of Southern California, vii, xvii

V

veal, grades of, 26
Veterans Administration, 153
Veterans Administration loans, 154
vitamins, 22
Voorhis, Jerry, vi, 47

W

Wall Street Journal, 127
warrants, 124
Washington, D.C., vi, 110
Washington Heights Federal Savings and Loan Association of New York, vii, 142

Westchester, 157
White, George, 38
White, Helen, vi, 8, 56, 72
Wilde, Oscar, 19
Williams, J. R., vi, 5
Women's Bureau of U. S. Dept. of Labor, 183
Women's Division of the Institute of Life Insurance, xv
Workmen's Compensation Law, 104
World War II, 127, 157, 158

Y

York, Herman H., vii, 157
Youngman, Burton L., vi

The Mallory Library